In a Heartbeat

To my friend, Jenny.
May God bless you!
Kim
1-12-11

In a Heartbeat

✦

A Baby's Heart,
A Surgeon's Hands,
A Life of Miracles

Written by Kimberly Russell

iUniverse, Inc.
New York Lincoln Shanghai

In a Heartbeat
A Baby's Heart, A Surgeon's Hands, A Life of Miracles

iUniverse books may be ordered through booksellers or by contacting:

iUniverse
2021 Pine Lake Road, Suite 100
Lincoln, NE 68512
www.iuniverse.com
1-800-Authors (1-800-288-4677)

In a Heartbeat is based on a true story. Some names have been changed to protect identities.
In a Heartbeat is written for reading pleasure only. It should not be used for medical reference or advice.
All Scripture references are from the King James Version and are used under public domain.
Lyrics for the hymns "I Am Jesus' Little Lamb," by Henrietta L. von Hayn; "Jesus Loves Me," by Anna B. Warner; and "Praise God from Whom All Blessings Flow," by Thomas Ken, are used under public domain.

ISBN-13: 978-0-595-39771-6 (pbk)
ISBN-13: 978-0-595-84178-3 (ebk)
ISBN-10: 0-595-39771-9 (pbk)
ISBN-10: 0-595-84178-3 (ebk)

Printed in the United States of America

In honor of my parents, Rev. Larry and Betty Vinton,
for the spiritual and physical care they have given me over the years.
Thank you, Mom and Dad, for teaching me that Jesus, my Savior, is always with me!

Contents

Foreword

"This book is an excellent portrayal of the productive, full life of a patient born with uncorrectable heart disease. It should be helpful to any family who has lived or is living with a loved one with congenital heart disease and is an excellent reminder that life can be well lived even in the face of severe medical problems."

Michael McConnell, M.D.
Sibley Heart Center Cardiology
Associate Clinical Professor of Pediatrics, Emory University School of Medicine
Assistant Clinical Professor of Medicine, Emory University School of Medicine
Codirector Emory/Sibley Adult Congenital Cardiac Clinic

Preface

I wrote *In a Heartbeat* with the anticipation of helping parents and families of children with congenital heart defects and other chronic illnesses. By sharing my journey of living with a congenital heart defect, I hope to make their pilgrimage a little easier.

Acknowledgments

Thank you to all of my family and friends who have been supportive and enthusiastic about the writing of this book. I could not have done it without you!

Thank you to my husband, Tom, for your love, encouragement, and confidence; my daughter, Stephanie Faithauer, for all of your love, support, and help; my parents, Larry and Betty Vinton, for helping me re-create the memories and for sharing your perspectives as parents; Rev. Larry Zahn, Rev. Fred Piepenbrink, Rev. Larry Vinton for reviewing the devotions for biblical accuracy; Diana Piepenbrink, April Forshee, Amy Cain, Mary Inman, Ann Warner, Sharon Wood, Jackie Villani, Melissa Bernandino, Terrie Russell for reading and/or editing my work; cardiologists Dr. Robert Franch, retired from Emory University, and Dr. Carole Warnes of Mayo Clinic; and Melanie Bazil at the Conrad R. Lam Archives.

A special note of gratitude to Dr. Michael McConnell of Emory University for all of your time, encouragement, enthusiasm, and guidance.

Chapter One

On July 19, 1960, Kimberly, now ten days old, was sleeping quietly in her crib as her mother, Betty, finished all of the work she had set out to do before the guests arrived. The dishes were done, the furniture was polished, and the floors were swept to perfection. Betty nodded to herself. Everything was just right. Soon her husband's aunt and uncle would be arriving. It's time to get myself ready, she thought.

Betty bathed and was putting the last few touches on her coarse, chestnut hair when Larry, her husband and childhood sweetheart, came looking for her. "They're here, Honey!" he announced. "By the way, you look great!" He gave his precious wife a special wink to remind her of his never-ending love.

"It's exciting to show off our new baby girl, isn't it?" Betty remarked as she grinned and beamed with pride. Her words fell on deaf ears as Larry went to answer the door. As Betty considered how exciting it really was, she remembered how thankful they were to have another child, let alone a daughter. The tall, slender mother leaned against the bathroom door as the memories came flooding back.

Betty and Larry were married the day after Betty graduated from high school. It was a beautiful wedding. They each had four attendants standing up with them. Betty's long, white, flowing dress hung to the floor. Her veil covered her face, and her train followed her up the aisle to her groom. The weather was warm and sunny. More than five hundred people were able to be with them on their special day. The wedding picture was still vivid in her memory.

One and a half years later, their bouncing baby boy, Brent, made his appearance into the world. He was a cute, happy little guy with big round cheeks and locks of blond hair. His eyes radiated as he giggled at almost anything, and his appetite was never lacking. As a toddler he liked almost any food, but soup was one of his favorites because it was something fun to pour, including onto his own head. No! Life was never dull after Brent was born. And Larry and Betty loved every moment. This had been a dream for both of them—to be married with children.

Two years later Betty joyfully discovered she was pregnant again. When she shared the news with Larry, he too was bursting with excitement. His head began to fill with all of the things that they would need to do. First, they needed to tell Brent that he was going to be a big brother. After he understood what that meant, his things could be moved to the "big brother" bedroom, where there was a twin bed. Training him to use it should not take long. Next, the proud father needed to get all of the baby clothes out of storage. Betty would unpack and wash them, including the diapers. Diapers? The busy father stopped in his tracks as if the thought had just hit him for the first time. A baby? We're really having a baby!

His mind raced into a flurry…a real baby! Would it be a girl? Or would it be a boy? What kind of big brother would Brent be? Definitely a protective one. He was a very thoughtful little guy. It would be fun to watch two children so close in age grow up together.

While the father-to-be contemplated all of those issues, Betty's enthusiasm also overflowed. Gradually she began focusing more and more earnestly on the gender of the anticipated baby. The pregnant mom had always imagined how fun it would be to have a girl. Girls could be dressed up as little ladies in frilly, lacy party outfits, and their hair could be styled so many cute ways. The farther into the pregnancy she got, the more excited she became! Of course, she would be happy no matter what God decided to give them. She and Larry both took confidence in Romans 8:28, "All things work together for good to them that love God, to them who are the called according to his purpose." But a girl would be so much fun!

On September 7, 1959, God did work all things together for good in a way that was totally unexpected. Baby Brad was born with hydrocephalus, an abnormality in which fluid collects in the brain. The condition was such that the baby's life would be very short, in fact, only four hours long. After taking time to comprehend the situation, the troubled parents immediately called their pastor.

The moments of sorrow and anguish were great. While waiting for their pastor, the struggling parents talked between themselves. Larry stroked the baby's cheek and held his wife's hand, as his mind wandered to what he had learned from his pastor in adult Bible information class.

"You know," he said, "I am so thankful that we have taken the Bible instruction class. The verses from John 3:16–17 keep revolving through my mind."

They recited the verses together: "For God so loved the world, that he gave his only begotten Son, that whosoever believeth in him should not perish, but have everlasting life. For God sent not his Son into the world to condemn the world; but that the world through him might be saved."

Pastor Martin walked through the door and into the room while Betty and Larry were in deep thought. He greeted each of them with a warm hug and handshake before the sad parents began sharing their news with him. "There is nothing they can do!" Betty sighed as tears filled her eyes. Before she could stop herself, the tears were running in a steady stream down her face. "This precious baby only has a short time on this earth, probably hours."

Pastor Martin expressed his sympathy. Not wanting to waste any time, he began by placing the sign of the cross both on the baby's head and on his heart as a sign of God's redeeming grace and faithfulness. Pouring a very small amount of water on the head of the sleeping infant, the minister announced, "Brad Duane Vinton, I baptize thee in the name of the Father, and of the Son, and of the Holy Ghost. Amen." In a heartbeat their lives were changed forever, as God took Brad and placed him in the arms of Jesus to live and remain with him forever. What a blessing that Brad could go immediately to heaven for all eternity! Yet how heartbreaking it was to leave the hospital without a baby!

Both of the young parents were deeply affected by the loss of their second son, but Betty had taken it the hardest. She was very quiet and mostly sad. Larry was very concerned about her, so he waited only a short time to begin asking Betty about having another baby. "We can't continue to dwell on what happened. Brad is in heaven. We need to use this experience to bring glory to God, and that can include having more children. The doctor told us that there was no physical explanation for Brad's death. Every pregnancy and birth is different. There was nothing we could have done differently to prevent what happened." After sharing his thoughts with his precious wife and reminding her of the doctor's words, he asked her to at least think about it. Betty finally consented after only a few weeks.

Not much time passed before Betty suspected that she had yet one more "little bun in the oven." After visiting the doctor for the confirmation of her suspicions, the tall, slight wife and mother went home and fixed a special dinner for her husband and her three-year-old son.

Brent didn't really understand what the excitement was all about, since there was no visual evidence. However, Larry's enthusiasm was overwhelming. As soon as the announcement was made, he gave his wife a great big bear hug and started planning phone calls to both sets of parents. The father's outward display of joy quickly spilled over into Betty's heart and brought back her love for life. Soon she was on the phone proudly telling her parents and Larry's parents that another grandchild was on the way.

As time progressed, Betty was thankful that this pregnancy was much easier than the others. The morning sickness was not nearly as intense as it had been with her other two children. The feeling of nausea was usually gone within an hour of waking, and Betty was not nearly as tired. Her stomach was not as large as it had been before either. One by one she thought about all of the differences between the pregnancies. The more she thought the more nervous she became. Everything was okay, wasn't it? Immediately she called the doctor's office for an appointment.

"Everything is fine," Dr. Joe Bernier, the family doctor, assured the anxious mother. "It is understandable that you are feeling cautious with this pregnancy because of your previous experience. That is normal and okay. If you have any other concerns, please do not hesitate to call. That is why we are here. Call any-time. It is better for you to know for sure that all is well than to sit and worry."

"Okay. Thanks!" Betty felt relieved that the doctor was not concerned.

As Dr. Bernier placed his hand on the door to exit the room, he turned to face Betty. "And by the way, I've been thinking about something that I wanted to tell you. The hospital's policy is that you cannot hold your baby for quite some time after birth. I plan to override that rule and let you hold the baby as soon as possi-ble. You deserve it."

Betty swelled with excitement. "Oh, thank you so much. That will be some-thing to look forward to."

Chapter Two

Betty woke up unusually early in the morning. She felt fidgety and somewhat nauseous. Getting up so as not to disturb Larry, who would have to go to work in a few hours, the twenty-two-year-old mother began to pace. Something just didn't seem right. Her back ached and she could not get comfortable, no matter what. Finally she decided to call her husband's Aunt Ellen, who was working the hospital switchboard. It would not hurt to call her at such an early hour.

"Aunt Ellen, this is Betty. How are you?"

"I'm fine, Honey. What are you doing up this early?"

"I'm not feeling well. I just wanted someone to talk to."

"Sure, what's wrong? Oh, I'm sorry, can you hold on a minute so I can get the other line?"

"Yes."

"Okay. Thanks."

While Ellen was gone, Betty talked herself into calming down a little. Having lower back pain, did not mean that there was something wrong with her pregnancy. The baby was not due for another three weeks. Everything would be just fine! *She hoped.*

Ellen was gone only a short time. "Now, what's going on?"

"Well," the pain-ridden mother explained, "I'm somewhat nauseous and very fidgety. My back hurts so much that I can't get in a comfortable position."

"When is your baby due?"

"Not for another three weeks."

"Are there any other problems? Bleeding? Is there cramping in your lower stomach or anything like that?" Ellen tried to help, while feeling a twinge of concern.

"No. Nothing like that. The baby's not due for another four weeks. Since we lost Brad last year when he was only three hours old, I'm afraid something might be going wrong with this baby." Betty began to sniffle.

"Now, wait a minute. Let's think this through. Have you been to the doctor lately?" Ellen was reaching for every explanation she could, even though she had her own suspicions.

"Yes, I was there last week. He said everything is fine. Oh, my goodness!" Betty had a sudden feeling of fluid on her legs. "I had better go."

"Okay, but" was all Ellen could say before Betty hung up. "Oh, my. I hope everything is okay," Betty thought.

As Betty hung up the phone, she began to feel a bit of pressure in her stomach. She headed for the bathroom, while calling out for her husband.

Larry came running to her. "What's the matter? Is something wrong?"

"My water broke. We had better get to the hospital! I can feel the downward pressure of the baby's head."

Larry looked at Betty in panic. He went through a mental checklist of what he was supposed to do. They had carefully planned it all out, so that everything would be done in a quick, orderly fashion. All of that preparation did the stunned father no good. He could barely remember what to do.

"Go, Honey, and hurry. I can feel the baby's head." Betty tried to remain calm as she called out from the bathroom. "We've got to hurry. Call the hospital and then take Brent over to the neighbor's house. I'll be right here when you get back."

That was all it took to put the shocked father into action. Betty could only watch as Larry called his work supervisor to tell him he would not be in and then called the hospital. Then he took Brent to their next-door neighbor's house. When he came back from the neighbor's house, he snatched up everything he thought they would need and loaded up the car. Within a very short time, they were on their way to the hospital. Midland Hospital was not far away, but the ride gave Betty opportunity to ponder her concern about her unborn baby.

The ride went very smoothly, and the excited father dropped his wife off where the nurses were waiting at the front door. After parking the car, he walked into the maternity ward to find his wife. As he entered the restricted hallway, the nurses began congratulating him. "You have a little girl!" they announced excitedly.

It took a few seconds for him to realize what they were telling him. All at once a big grin spread across his face. "A girl? So where are they? Are they okay?"

"Both of them are just fine. Your wife is right down that hallway on the left."

Larry took off in the direction the nurse had showed him. When he came around the corner, the happy husband found his tired wife crying. "Larry, we have a girl! She weighs seven pounds one ounce and is a full 20 inches long. It's a girl!"

"Betty, Larry, congratulations!" the doctor exclaimed as he entered the room holding the newborn in his short stocky arms. "Your daughter is beautiful!" He went directly to the beaming mother and handed her the little bundle. "What a blessing! A healthy baby girl! Do you have a name picked out?"

Betty grinned from ear to ear. "Kimberly Jean."

The doctor shook Larry's hand after giving the new mother a hug. Then he flipped open the patients' medical charts and made a few notations that mother and baby were doing well. Closing them back up, he looked into the eyes of both mother and father. "I'm going home now. If you need anything, and I do mean *anything*, just give me a call. Again, congratulations!" The doctor turned to exit the room, elated that all had gone well. The doctor was smiling so wide that one would have thought it was his own child, or at least his granddaughter. This family had had some very trying times in the past year, and he was thankful that the hard part was over for them.

As soon as the family physician disappeared from the doorway, Larry hugged his wife. "I'm going to bring Brent up this evening. Last time we built up the excitement of being a big brother and then didn't bring a baby home. He was only two and a half, but it still affected him."

"Yes, seeing this baby will be good for him," Betty agreed.

Chapter Three

Just as quickly as Betty's memories had started, they came to an abrupt end. She heard the doorbell ring and felt Larry touch her arm and call her name. She shook her head, which helped her realize that she had just relived the past four years in a matter of seconds. She hurried across the hall to greet Larry's aunt and uncle while whispering a prayer of thanksgiving to her Lord. How glad she and her husband were to show family and friends the baby girl God had chosen to give them!

"Hello!" Larry's red-headed aunt greeted Betty and her tall, handsome husband. "How are you?"

"Hi! We're fine. How are the two of you? It is so good to see you." Larry shook hands with his Uncle Harrison and hugged his Aunt Florine.

"We couldn't put off seeing our grand-niece we keep hearing about." Aunt Florine winked and chuckled, as Brent came running into the living room.

"And how are you, Brent?" Uncle Harrison inquired of the animated little three-year-old.

"I'm fine! Guess what? We have a new sister!" Brent was eager to tell about his new sister. "She sleeps a lot though, so I don't get to play with her very much. She only wakes up to eat."

"Oh?" Aunt Florine answered quizzically, listening intently to all the little guy had to say.

Betty looked down at Brent. "He doesn't understand that babies only eat and sleep. He thought he was getting a new playmate."

Florine grinned in understanding, as they all sat down in the living room.

"Brent, should we get Kim and show her to them now?" Betty asked.

"Yes, can we? Do you want to see her, Aunt Florine and Uncle Harrison?"

"That would be great! Will you let us hold her too?" Florine fed his enthusiasm as she patted his shoulder.

"Sure!" the proud brother agreed.

Brent followed his mother into his new sister's room. The mother and son wrapped her in a small blanket and carried her to the living room. "See, Aunt Florine and Uncle Harrison!" Brent exclaimed excitedly. "She has yellow hair and itsy-bitsy toes and fingers. She's our new baby!" Brent was pleased as punch. Then he began to explain to his great aunt and uncle about "how babies work." They chuckled and winked at each other. Having raised two of their own children, they were very familiar with "how babies work."

Florine stretched out her arms to take the light blond, curly-headed baby carefully from Betty's hands. How exciting—her new grandniece! And only two weeks old! The proud aunt turned the small, sleeping child toward her, so that her husband could see too. As soon as she started unwrapping the baby from the blanket, fear gripped her heart.

Florine placed the baby in her lap, trying not to show concern, and began to look over every part of the little body. Uncle Harrison looked at her questioningly. She gave him one of those looks that can convey a message from wife to husband without anyone noticing. Her look told him not to look alarmed or to do anything that let the new parents know she was concerned.

Harrison smiled at her in understanding and commented on how precious newborns are. Then he kept the parents entertained in conversation, as his wife did some further investigating.

Florine pulled all the blankets back, as if she was excited about seeing all the grandniece's body parts. The more the aunt saw, the more her suspicions were aroused. The fingernails? Yes. The toenails? Yes. The bottoms of her feet? Yes. There were so many signs that it made her ill to think about it. Hadn't Betty noticed that Kim's skin had a bluish tint to it?

As a nurse she had been in similar situations of knowing something was wrong but not having the right to say anything about it. Being in this position was difficult. So as not to startle anyone or give reason for alarm, the concerned aunt began asking questions. "How has Kim been doing?" she asked.

"Fine," Larry and Betty both confirmed at the same time.

Betty was eager to tell more. "Kim is a good baby. She seldom cries. She sleeps a lot. Sometimes I even have to wake her up to feed her. She was born three weeks early though, so she is probably trying to catch up."

Florine shook her head in understanding. This was the perfect chance to express her impression. "When is her next checkup?"

"The doctor wants to see her in two weeks for a one-month checkup."

Florine smiled and nodded her head. "I think you should take her in tomorrow so the doctor can see her. It's not good for a baby this age to sleep as much as you say she does, especially if she is not eating properly. Being inactive and not crying can cause fluid to get into her lungs, which can lead to pneumonia. Something about her color just doesn't seem right."

Both parents listened intently, a slight frown of concern appearing on their foreheads. They gave each other a sideways glance. Betty was the first to speak. "That thought never crossed our minds. But it makes sense. I'll give the doctor a call tomorrow and see if we can get an immediate appointment."

Florine felt relief pass over her entire body. The conversation had gone well. Betty and Larry were concerned and somewhat anxious, but not panicked. Betty even agreed to take Kim to the doctor. That was exactly what she had hoped for. Florine knew Dr. Joe Bernier was a good physician. Her grandniece would get the best of care.

Chapter Four

Perplexed, Betty waited in the small, pristinely white room with Kimberly held tightly in her arms. She realized they might have to wait a while since they had made their appointment with Dr. Bernier that very morning. The tired, apprehensive mother was still wondering why she was here. But since Florine was a nurse and a member of the family, taking her advice was the right thing to do.

After about forty-five minutes, Betty heard the doctor in the hallway right outside the door. He was refreshing himself on the events of Kimberly's birth—her weight, length, and all of the other significant notations. The round, jolly man swung the door open and greeted them cheerfully. "Good morning! I'm sorry you had to wait so long. We had a couple of minor emergencies this morning."

"Good morning, Dr. Joe. We just really appreciate that you were able to fit us in this morning. Thank you." Betty responded with a smile of her own.

"It's good to see you again. How is that baby girl?"

Dr. Joe laid the chart on his desk and turned to visit with Betty. "Is everything going okay?" The doctor slowly reached down to take the newborn. His strong, solid arms nearly swallowed the infant. "You weren't scheduled to come for two more weeks. Let's see." Dr. Bernier took a second glance at Kimberly's chart for a birth date. "She is not quite two weeks old."

"No, she isn't," Betty replied, "but Larry's aunt was over last night. She doesn't think Kimberly should sleep so much. She also mentioned something about her skin color."

"Let's have a look." Dr Joe carefully removed the tightly wrapped blankets from around the little girl. At first sight, a lump lodged in his throat. His face turned ashen, as his stomach filled with knots. Something was wrong. He wasn't sure what.

Slowly the red-haired, concerned doctor laid the sleeping baby on the examination table. No words came from the physician as he examined every inch of the baby's body. First, he looked closely at her fingernails, then her toenails. Next, he looked carefully at her lips, holding her fingers close to her mouth to compare colors. Then he checked the bottoms of her feet.

The room was so quiet and still. There was no sound, no movement. A pin drop could have been heard.

After completing the body exam, the doctor slid his stethoscope from around his neck. Continuing quietly, he listened to four different areas on her chest. Then he slowly and gently flipped the baby over to listen some more on her back. Taking a moment to think, he took in a deep breath, nodded, and turned to Betty, trying not to reveal his intense concern.

Tears came to his eyes as he looked up at her and exhaled slowly. "Betty, I need to look some things up in my office. In the meantime, could you please call Larry and get him to come over?"

"Yes," she hesitated. "Is there something wrong?"

"Well, I'm not really sure what the situation is. Let me do my research, and I'll be back when Larry gets here." The doctor turned to go to his office, as thoughts raced through his head. Maybe I'm wrong, he thought. I'm only a family doctor.

After flipping through several of his medical books and reading about the symptoms Kim was having, Dr. Bernier called a pediatric cardiologist at Henry Ford Hospital in Detroit. As he read a full description of the symptoms to the head cardiologist there, the general practitioner realized there was no way he could be wrong. Kim definitely had some sort of heart defect. The question was—what kind?

Dr. Joe answered all of the cardiologist's questions as best as he could, while the man on the other end of the phone tried to piece all of the information together. Then the feared news came. He listened intently as the cardiologist confirmed his diagnosis. Kimberly most likely had a problem with the structure of her heart that caused a lack of oxygen in her body. This explained why her lips, nails, and the bottoms of her feet were so blue.

"Dr. Bernier, are you there?" the cardiologist asked.

"Yes, I'm here. Please forgive me for letting my mind wander. The members of this family are personal friends of mine. The baby they delivered a year ago died when he was only four hours old. How am I going to tell them that their newborn daughter is not as healthy as we first thought? There were no signs of any kind immediately after birth."

"Don't second guess yourself, Joe. Some defects cannot be detected until a few weeks and even months after birth. I'm just sorry that you have to be the one to tell them. But you have picked the right hospital to call. We have an excellent pediatric cardiology department. Dr. Robert Ziegler, in particular, is one of the most knowledgeable cardiologists in congenital heart defects. If you will hold on for one moment, I'll see if I can get you an appointment with him."

The phone went silent for only a moment. "Dr. Bernier?"

"Yes."

"The appointment is for the day after tomorrow. Have them come prepared to stay overnight. Most likely we will have to do a heart catheterization to diagnose the exact defect. In the meantime have them take the baby home and watch her carefully. If anything changes, have them come here immediately. They should watch for signs of labored breathing or a change in skin color."

"Thank you so much! You have been most helpful and encouraging."

"You're welcome. Please let me know if you need anything else or if there are any changes. That way I can have a team of cardiologists ready for their arrival. If I am not here, my secretary will know how to find me."

"Okay. Thanks again!"

As Dr. Bernier hung up the receiver, he felt much better knowing more about Kim's condition. He stepped into the hallway to see if Larry had arrived yet. Peaking through the crack in the door, he saw the anxious father with his baby girl nestled on his shoulder.

The plump doctor took a deep breath, willed himself to be strong, then knocked and entered the room where the curious parents were patiently waiting.

"Hi, Larry," he said in a friendly, yet serious tone. "I'm glad that you could come. Florine did the right thing by having you come in. Her suspicions were well placed." Dr. Joe looked down and took a slightly deep breath before going on.

Looking back up and into the eyes of each parent, he went on somewhat hesitantly. "Kimberly's skin color is not right, especially on her nail beds, her lips, and the bottoms of her feet. At first I thought maybe she was ill with pneumonia or some such lung problem. But the blueness together with the rather loud-sounding murmur in her chest leads me to believe that her heart is involved." The physician continued to talk steadily to keep the alarmed parents from asking questions until he had given them all of the information he had. "I spoke with a cardiologist at Henry Ford Hospital in Detroit. He is concerned that Kim might have a congenital heart defect, congenital meaning from birth. He scheduled an appointment for you for the day after tomorrow. I realize that Henry Ford is a long drive from here, but their pediatric cardiology department is one of the best."

"Day after tomorrow?" Larry blurted out. "That is way too long."

Dr. Joe tried to reassure the parents. "I spent quite some time on the phone to figure out what to do. This was the cardiologist's recommendation, so we need to have the confidence that he is making the right decision. Remember, they are the best group of cardiologists in the state."

Larry was not satisfied. "And what are we supposed to do in the meantime? Watch her die before our very eyes? Take the chance that our little girl suddenly needs urgent medical attention and hope we will have time to drive two and a half hours to get her to the doctors that can help her? Think about that!"

Dr. Joe knew Larry was caught up in grief and frustration. It was nothing personal, just fear of what would happen next. "Larry, I *am* very sorry. I know this is frightening for both of you, but the cardiologist was very comfortable with his decision. Thursday is the soonest they could get you in. He also told me to have you take Kim home and watch her very carefully. If she shows any signs of labored breathing or her skin begins to become a darker shade of blue, call me immediately. I will call the cardiologist while you are on your way."

Betty broke into tears. As she sobbed, the doctor placed his hand on her shoulder to give her what comfort he could. "Betty, it could not have been prevented. I am just so sorry that you are going through this after all you went through with Brad. But you must believe me! You did nothing to contribute to this!"

The shaken mother could not think of any questions. She gathered all of their belongings and began to walk out of the office. With Kim in one arm, she turned and hugged the doctor as tears slowly trickled down his cheeks. "Joe, thank you. You too have to remember there is nothing you could have done. Everything will be okay. It is in God's hands. Larry loves his daughter very much. This is hard for both of us, but especially for him. We'll call you if we need to."

Larry took the infant from her mother's arms and squeezed her tightly as they walked out to the car.

Chapter Five

On the way home from the doctor's office, Betty and Larry did not engage in conversation. They were each caught up in their own thoughts. Finally Larry spoke. "We should call our parents later on this afternoon."

Betty agreed.

"Okay, Mom. I'll tell him. We love you and Dad too." Betty hung up the phone. As she turned to Larry, who stood next to her, tears exploded from her eyes and sobs escaped from her throat. At least she had been strong for both sets of parents over the phone.

Larry held Betty lovingly for several minutes. Then he gently pulled back from her to look her directly in the face. He loved her so much. "I love you," he said, looking into her eyes while holding her hands. "Maybe it would be a good idea for us to take our own advice. We are imagining only the worst. Until the cardiologists can tell us exactly what is wrong, we need to watch and pray. We have two children who desperately need our love and attention. That is where we need to place our focus."

"Thank you, Dear," Betty said, thankful for having such a caring husband. She hugged Larry once again and kissed him on the cheek. "Thank you for being strong enough to help me stay strong too. You're a good husband, and I love you very much."

"I called Pastor Martin when we got home," Larry told his wife. "He would be glad for us to come over in a little while. Let's have dinner and go over about seven."

"Good idea. I'll fix something quick."

Pastor Martin was a kind, loving, gentle soul who had a special gift for helping people. He always had the right thing to say at just the right time. The small-framed, balding minister worked at his desk while waiting for Betty and Larry to arrive.

Soon there was a knock on his door. "Hi, Larry and Betty," he greeted them. "How are you doing?" he asked as he shook Larry's hand and gave Betty a quick hug. Their red, puffy eyelids and blotched faces revealed that a trial had come into their lives.

"We're doing pretty well, but as you can see, we're both upset." Larry confirmed the pastor's thoughts.

"Oh," the pastor commented as he turned his chair to face his troubled parishioners. "Why don't you have a seat, and we will begin with a prayer."

The young couple eased into the soft, comfortable armchairs that he offered. They folded their hands and bowed their heads as the pastor began. "Dear Lord God, heavenly Father, thank you for this opportunity to come together as fellow Christians to help bear each other's burdens. Please place thy loving arms around these young people, reminding them that thou hast promised to be with us always. Bless them as they share their troubled hearts. Guide us all, and bless our time together that the words we say and the thoughts we share may be pleasing in thy sight. Give us an extra measure of faith to deal with the problems before us. In the name of Jesus Christ, our Lord and Savior. Amen."

"Thank you, Pastor," Larry said appreciatively. "Sometimes it is easy to forget that Jesus promises to be *with* us always."

The pastor grinned shyly. "Yes, that happens to all of us, I'm afraid."

Pastor Martin listened attentively as Larry gave Betty a relaxed, comforting smile and began to share the events of the day. Slowly one tear after the other leaked from the troubled father's eyes and slipped slowly down his cheeks. He began to sob and was unable to finish.

Betty continued where Larry had left off, her bright green eyes becoming clouded. "Our family doctor thinks that Kim has some sort of structural malformation in her heart." She sniffed. "He can hear a loud murmur, but he doesn't know exactly what is causing it. Without the necessary cardiac equipment, he can't tell any more than that. He has made an appointment for us with a pediatric cardiologist at Henry Ford Hospital. Tests will be run Thursday, one of which may require an overnight stay, so we should be home sometime Friday."

The pastor/friend sat somewhat stunned. Slowly he reached for his Bible. God provided so much comfort and encouragement in his Word. Pastor Martin flipped through the pages, looking for some of his favorite Bible verses.

"Our heavenly Father has given instructions to his children for times such as these," he began. "Proverbs 3:5 reads, 'Trust in the Lord with all thine heart; and lean not unto thine own understanding.' In Psalm 46:10 God tells us, 'Be still, and know that I am God.'

"The triune God who created everything from the beginning, the only true God who has control of all things, the same God who planned out our salvation wants us to be still and trust. What does that mean? It means that God wants us to search through his precious Word to find his answers to our daily trials and struggles. He also wants us to trust that he is in control. He knows our problems and already has a plan worked out for them. God always has a reason and a purpose for everything. So instead of offering our own answers to our own problems or making judgments as the disciples did when they thought a son born blind was the result of a specific sin (John 9:13), we wait. We wait and trust the Lord.

"Our God is all-knowing, all powerful, gracious, kind, loving, and merciful. We are to trust that he will take care of us in every situation. He wants us to trust his words in Psalm 46:1, 'God is our refuge and strength, a very present help in trouble.'"

The sincere, concerned minister went on to remind them of the song that they had long been singing to their children: "Jesus loves me, this I know, for the Bible tells me so. Little ones to him belong; they are weak, but he is strong." Yes, Jesus, their Savior, loved them very much and would be *with* them always. The very God that created heaven and earth was not just near them watching, not just sitting in the heavens knowing what was happening, but he was right here *with* them. He would work all things out according to his will and his perfect purpose.

The pastor continued to remind the parents of God's care. "We know from John 3:16 in the Holy Scriptures that 'God so loved the world, that he gave his only begotten Son, that whosoever believeth in him should not perish, but have everlasting life.' God has so much love and compassion for all of his children!" Then the pastor closed with prayer.

Very refreshed, the young couple thanked the pastor and went home to prepare for their trip to the hospital.

Two days later, on July 22, Larry and Betty dropped Brent off at his grandparents' house. Then they left with Kim for the road trip to the cardiology clinic at the hospital.

The weather was nice for traveling. The sun was shining, with a few clouds dancing in the sky. The temperature was hot, but not unbearably so. Riding in the car was relaxing, even though the reason for the trip was unnerving. The couple made small talk to keep themselves occupied while Kimberly slept.

Arriving safely, the couple got out of the car and looked at the building they were about to enter. The hospital was made of red brick with ornately decorated cement enclosing the windows on every side. "This is a big place," Betty commented, looking up floor by floor.

"It sure is," said Larry as they strode toward the front entrance.

Entering through the revolving doors, the young couple got directions to the cardiac unit. They held hands, while following the path of brown floor tiles that the receptionist had shown them. After finding the elevator, they nervously made their way to the thirteenth floor of the hospital. There was still half an hour to spare, so they looked around a little, trying to confirm in their minds that this was, indeed, the right place to get help for their daughter.

As they walked down the hall, hand in hand, they spotted a large yellow and white sign that in big blue letters read "CARDIOLOGY." "This must be where we need to go," Larry said as he pointed to the sign. Arriving at the main waiting area for cardiology, the anxious parents sat down. A man dressed in a white coat appeared at the desk to talk to the receptionist. Larry thought he heard his name mentioned in the dialogue between the doctor and his secretary.

"Excuse me," Larry said without hesitation. "My name is Larry Vinton. Is this where we are to register for a cardiology appointment?"

"Why, yes." The doctor held out his hand. "Hi! I'm Dr. Robert Ziegler. I was just asking if you had arrived. Our cardiology staff had to come in early today, so we decided to begin as soon as you arrived."

Larry shook the doctor's hand. "This is my wife, Betty." The doctor shook her hand in turn and then looked inside the blanket that the charming mother held.

"This must be Kimberly," the doctor guessed.

"Yes," the proud mother replied with a grin.

"Do you have any other children?" the doctor asked.

"Yes, we have a three-year-old son who is staying with his grandparents."

The doctor smiled at both mother and father. "If you're ready, let's go into my office and get started."

The couple followed the gentle, mild-mannered man down a corridor to his small office. The room was spacious, but rather plain. The walls were beige, and the floor was covered with neutral-colored tile. The chairs were not extraordinary either.

Offering them each a comfortable, straight-backed chair, the doctor began to inquire about Kimberly's birth and health. "Tell me everything you can, and I will ask questions when you are finished," he told them.

The proud mother and father recounted how easy the birth had been and that the doctor had pronounced her a healthy baby girl. Then they related how much Kimberly slept and how a relative pointed out the bluish tint of her skin. "Dr. Bernier seemed really concerned that there might be some sort of structural problem with her heart," Betty related, trying hard to keep the wetness in her eyes at bay. Slowly the water trickled down her cheeks.

"Hmm!" The doctor had a few different thoughts running through his well-educated mind. "Has she been eating okay?"

"We have to wake her to get her to eat, and even then it seems as though she works really hard at sucking and tires quickly," Betty informed him. "When she does eat, she doesn't eat much."

As the cardiologist continued to think through the possibilities, he took the seven-pound infant from her mother's arms. Placing her on the exam table in the corner of the room, he said nothing as he poked, prodded, and listened. It reminded Betty of her visit to Dr. Bernier's office. The room was silent for many minutes. The Vintons held each other's hands as they waited quietly in anticipation.

When the doctor had heard and seen all he needed to, he handed Kimberly back to her father. "Judging from Kimberly's color and the sound of her heartbeat, I would guess that the diagnosis that Dr. Bernier gave you is accurate," the cardiologist began. "However, to know exactly what is wrong, we will need to run a few tests. We'll start with a blood test. Then she will have an X ray and electrocardiogram this morning. We have also tentatively scheduled a heart catheterization…"

"I'm sorry to interrupt, Dr. Ziegler," Larry interjected anxiously, "but could you please explain what kind of tests those are? We are not at all familiar with cardiology terms. All of this is new to us and rather overwhelming."

"Please forgive me!" the heart doctor apologized. "Sometimes I get so caught up on working through the case in my head that I forget to explain what I mean. You are probably familiar with the X ray." Both parents shook their heads yes, so the cardiologist went on. "In the electrocardiogram, also known as an EKG, we will place rubber cuffs around Kimberly's ankles and wrists. These cuffs are hooked to wires from the EKG machine, which will record electrical impulses sent to the heart to regulate its rhythms from all four chambers. It takes approximately ten minutes from start to finish. It is not at all invasive."

"Wow! Imagine that!" Larry was completely amazed at the technology the doctor described. The young father had been fascinated with mechanical things from the time he was a small child, often taking apart small appliances to see just how they worked. Then his face changed to somewhat of a frown. "Will any of this be painful for her?"

"No. The only thing that will bother her this morning is the blood test, and that will only feel like a pinch. She won't like it, but it will only take a couple minutes. Our nurses are very careful and precise, I promise you. Kimberly will not go through any pain unnecessarily."

The cardiologist allowed the couple to think for a few minutes about what he had said. It had been his intention to tell them that most likely a heart catheterization would need to be done in the afternoon. But seeing that they were already overwhelmed, he decided to cross that bridge if and when they needed to.

"Let's go out to the receptionist, and she will show you where you need to go first. Just remember that when all the tests are done, we will meet back here."

The parents nodded that they understood, but both were still speechless, trying to take in all he had told them.

Approaching the receptionist, the doctor began his request, "Mrs. Wood, could you please explain to Mr. and Mrs. Vinton the times and places of their testing appointments and how to get around the hospital?"

The middle-aged woman smiled and nodded in agreement.

"Thanks! I'll see you in a little while," the cardiologist confirmed to the parents.

Larry reached out his right hand in thankfulness for all the care the cardiologist had shown his family. "Yes," he said. "We'll be back later. Thank you."

The doctor had been right. Kimberly most certainly did not appreciate having her blood drawn, but she was calm and quiet as the three of them approached the X-ray department. It was a little difficult to find, but they arrived on time, and the test went quickly. Before they knew it, they were on their way to the electrocardiogram department.

The wait was not long there either. For this test, the eager mother and father were allowed to walk their daughter down to the door of the EKG room, but they were not allowed to enter it with Kim and the nurse. Anxiously the couple turned their tiny bundle over to the technician. While the medical worker swung the arms of the EKG machine over to the bed and wrapped the rubber straps around Kimberly's ankles and wrists, Larry peeked into the small room to try to get a concept of how this machine worked. The massive instrument filled the whole back wall and an area about five feet behind it. All of this large equipment was needed for a test on a tiny baby?

The technician interrupted the curious father's thoughts, asking both of the parents to step back as she shut the door. "No one can be in the room while the machine is running. It is very sensitive."

The reluctant but obedient parents moved nervously out of the way. Five minutes seemed like an eternity with their infant lying in a small, dark room all alone.

Their imaginations could run wild thinking of how scary it could be. But the test concluded without even so much as a peep from the little girl. When the nurse retrieved her, the mother and father found she had slept through the whole thing.

The EKG technician turned toward the couple and handed Kimberly to them. "Dr. Ziegler's receptionist called. After your next stop, you can go to lunch. The doctor would like to see you back in his office at one o'clock. He wants to have a little time to review all of the information they have gathered from the tests before he meets with you."

"Oh, good! We were getting kind of hungry, but we didn't know if we were going to have time to eat." Larry thanked the hospital worker.

Looking forward to lunch and their meeting with the doctor, the young couple held hands as they made their way to the hospital cafeteria. They were glad to have a few moments to sit and relax, all the while talking about the information the doctor had given them.

The Normal Heart

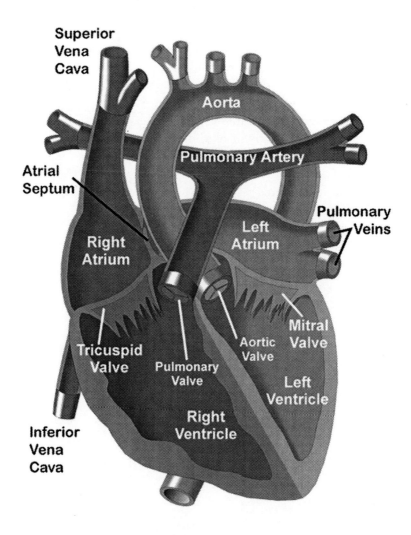

From the *Illustrated Field Guide to Congenital Heart Disease and Repair*
Courtesy of Scientific Software Solutions, Inc
(Used by permission)

Chapter Six

Promptly at one o'clock Dr. Ziegler rapped on his office door to let the Vintons know he was on his way in. They both looked very tired and nervous. This was the moment of truth.

"Were you able to fit in lunch?" the cardiologist inquired.

"Yes, thank you," Larry replied. "We were hungrier than we realized."

"Good. I am glad you got to do that." The cardiologist shuffled some papers on his desk and turned toward them. Leaning against the exam table, he began to tell the parents what the tests had revealed. "All of the test results are back, and we have looked at them thoroughly. I'd like to show you from a chart where we think Kim's defect is located."

Think? The question flitted through Larry's mind. *Our daughter has gone through all of this and you* think *you know what's wrong? Hmm!* But he kept silent as the cardiologist continued. "Let me start by showing you a chart of what a normal heart looks like. As you can see, a normal heart is divided into four sections, which act as pumps. They consist of two atria on top and two ventricles on the bottom." He wanted to begin with the basics of cardiology. This information would help Betty and Larry follow along. "Blood comes into the heart on the right side to get to the lungs for oxygenation. After it flows into the top right atrium, it goes through a valve right here." Dr. Ziegler pointed to the chart and continued. "That pumps it down into the right ventricle, which sends it down to the lungs."

The doctor pointed to the blood flow chart, showing them where each valve and pump was located and where the blood was flowing in and down.

"After the blood gets its oxygen from the lungs, it goes into the left atrium, down to the left ventricle, and back out to the body."

Larry stared at the chart for a moment. "Using this heart structure chart definitely makes following along easier."

The doctor nodded his head in agreement, paused, and then went on. "You can see from this diagram that there is a wall between the right and left atria and between the right and left ventricles. This keeps the oxygenated blood from mixing with the blood that has not yet been oxygenated, as it is processed to and from the lungs."

Larry looked at Betty. "Looking at this chart really makes you wonder how people can believe that everything evolved, instead of being made by our heavenly Creator, doesn't it? It's all so intricate and interconnected!"

The doctor listened to the brief discussion between the husband and wife. Then he continued. "The tests we have done indicate that Kimberly has a defect that is allowing oxygenated blood and unoxygenated blood to mix together before going out to the body. We suspect that she has a hole in the ventricular septum.

"To actually see Kimberly's defect and measure the blood flow through the heart, it would be best to do a heart catheterization. In this procedure a very small tube is inserted into an artery near the groin. Through this tube we run wires that have cameras at the end, allowing us to actually *see* the entire anatomy of the heart."

Larry placed an arm around Betty as they considered what this meant. They both began to shed tears.

Dr. Ziegler looked at them with compassion in his eyes. "Kimberly has something wrong. It is obvious from her blueness that she is not getting enough oxygen to her body. She needs help. This is the best test to figure out what to do for her."

The parents agreed, both shaking their heads. "We understand," Betty responded.

"You have my word that we will do our best to work quickly and carefully. For now, we need to get Kimberly admitted into the hospital. Her catheterization is scheduled for this afternoon, but she needs to stay all night to be monitored. One of our nurses has reserved a room for her. After you are settled, a catheterization technician will come and get her."

Betty and Larry rose to leave Dr. Ziegler's office. "Please take good care of her," Larry pleaded.

Dr. Ziegler shook Larry's hand and promised to do his best.

After the Vintons had "taken up residence" in Kimberly's hospital room, a nurse stepped in pushing a small cart. "We're ready for Kimberly," she announced. With a few tears and a couple of last-minute hugs, the mother and father placed Kim into the small bed.

"This should only take a little while," the hospital worker confirmed. "She will be back as soon as possible."

The troubled parents nodded in assent.

Chapter Seven

Betty and Larry were pacing the floor when the nurse came in pushing Kim's small bed. The worried parents were very glad to see her. Shortly afterwards Dr Ziegler walked in.

"Good afternoon," he greeted them as he shook their hands. "Kimberly did great!" Leaning against the wall, while adjusting his glasses, Dr. Ziegler started to talk about the test results. Then he reconsidered. "There isn't much space in this room, and Dr. Lam, our pediatric cardiology surgeon, is coming too. Would it be okay if we stepped across the hall to the conference room to review the test results?" He saw Betty looking longingly at her baby. "Kimberly will sleep for quite awhile. We'll leave both doors open if you like."

"I'd prefer that, if you don't mind," the quiet mother answered shyly.

When the focused group walked into the small conference room, the surgeon was already present. Leaning over the table, he greeted both parents. "Mr. Vinton, it is nice to meet you. I'm Dr. Conrad Lam." The kind, broad-shouldered surgeon shook Larry's hand. Then he nodded to Betty. "Mrs. Vinton, it is nice to meet you also. Thank you for allowing me to join you."

When they were all seated at one end of the eight-foot conference table, Dr. Ziegler pulled out his green folder of reference notes. After a moment of silence while he was trying to figure out how to start, he began speaking, his face friendly and serious at the same time. "After we reviewed all of the results from the procedures Kimberly had this morning, Dr. Lam and I both participated in her catheterization this afternoon."

Dr. Ziegler thumbed through a stack of papers and picked up a blood flow chart. It was a picture of a healthy heart showing each part with its function clearly labeled. It was very similar to the one he had used in their prior consultation. "Earlier in your visit, we discussed that a normal heart has four chambers: two on the top, the atria, and two on the bottom, the ventricles." He pointed at the chart, refreshing in their minds what they had learned earlier in the day.

Larry and Betty studied the chart. The cardiologist began pointing again, running his finger along the chart, reminding them how the heart worked.

"Kim's blueness indicates that she is not getting enough oxygen to her body. The question is why. What is causing the low-oxygen saturation?

"During the catheterization we found three problems. First, we discovered that Kimberly has no wall between her two bottom chambers. In fact, we are not sure whether there even is a right ventricle, because there are two inlets into the left ventricle. One of those inlets should have gone to the right ventricle. Since all of the in-flowing blood and the out-flowing blood are going through the same ventricle, the blood with oxygen and the oxygen-depleted blood are mixing. So the blood going out to her body has a reduced amount of oxygen. This is causing her to turn blue, tire quickly with exertion, and become easily fatigued.

"The second and third visible deformities are sort of interrelated. When we look at the blood flow chart of a normal heart, we see that there is one place where the blood flows into the heart and one place where it flows out. Kimberly's heart is not like that. She has two places where the blood comes in. In addition, the pulmonary artery, which lets blood flow from the ventricle down to the lungs, is slightly narrowed. So far those two abnormalities do not seem to be causing any distress or problems. They could with time, but that is just a wait-and-see situation."

The parents studied the chart, trying to let all the information sink into their bewildered minds. It was overwhelming and scary. They looked at each other, tears sitting in their eyes waiting to escape down their cheeks. Underneath the table they squeezed hands, each offering comfort and strength to the other.

Betty allowed the tears to flow down her cheeks, but she sat quietly and stared while the words "lean not unto thine own understanding" rotated in her mind over and over.

Larry could not listen anymore without trying to make sense of it all. His face showed deepening concern and frustration. "So what are we facing here? What kind of help is there for her? She obviously has to have help soon. Are you planning to do some sort of surgery?"

Dr. Ziegler looked sideways at Dr. Lam, while a slight frown crawled onto Dr. Lam's forehead. They both hated this type of meeting with parents. It was the worst part of their jobs—telling a young father and mother there is little to no hope for their baby. They didn't want to send them away in a state of despair, but they also had to tell them the truth. The surgeon hung his head slightly and slowly let out a long deep sigh. "No, not right now. Kimberly is much too small and weak. The risks are too high. Her heart is not even as big as a golf ball. It is almost impossible to operate on something so small and intricate. If possible, we would like to wait until Kim is as close as possible to age three before operating.

After she grows some, we would consider doing a fairly successful procedure called a Blalock-Taussig shunt, which was invented in 1944. This sixteen-year-old surgery would reroute a vein from her arm directly to her pulmonary artery, causing more oxygenated blood to get to her body. But right now Kim is too small. What we are hoping for is more time for her to grow."

The parents could not keep control of their emotions. Worry lines formed on their foreheads, as ripples of water poured from their eyes. Larry was the first to express his feelings. "This is so much to absorb! We are not nurses or doctors. How can you expect us to take care of our daughter at home? What if something goes wrong and we don't notice?"

Knowing that the mother and father were struggling, the surgeon broke in. "Before we go any further, why don't you take some time to think all of this through, and we will discuss it tomorrow before you go home. Keep a pad of paper and a pen handy. As you think of questions, write them down. In the morning I'll stop by before you go home and try to answer any questions." The soft-hearted surgeon knew that the cardiologist was struggling himself. Having to tell parents this kind of news was not easy.

"That is a good idea," Dr. Ziegler agreed.

Dr. Lam shook hands with the parents. "When I come, I will give you some information on the signs and conditions to watch for. If you even *think* something is changing, please call us immediately."

Betty breathed a sigh of relief. At least they would have some guidelines to go by. They knew so little and needed to know so much. "Can we keep this heart diagram?" she asked.

"Sure, that will be fine."

The next morning when the surgeon came by, he greeted them optimistically. "Good morning," Dr. Lam said, shaking Larry's hand. "How are you doing?"

Betty and Larry looked quite refreshed from a good night's sleep. "About the same, thank you," Larry announced. Then in desperation he looked directly at the surgeon. "Why can't you do *something*? It sounds as though we are taking our daughter home to let her die!"

Dr. Lam ran his fingers through his hair and gave the parents a sympathetic nod. With a calm, gentle voice, he began to explain. "That is not the case at all. At this hospital we treat each child as if he or she was our own. When difficult cases arise, like this one, several doctors collaborate about what to do. We do not make any decisions until we are all in agreement.

"In Kim's situation the decision was unanimous almost from the beginning. Kimberly is too small to survive the surgery. We're sending her home to grow so that she has a better chance of surviving the surgery.

"Could something happen to her before she grows enough for the surgery?" said Dr. Lam, echoing the parents' thoughts. "It is a very real possibility. One morning you could go to her room and find her dead in her crib. But if we do surgery now, it is a much greater possibility that she would die during surgery. We are not giving up on her; we are just letting her get as big as she can before we do anything. The bigger she is, the less the risk."

The surgeon reached over to Kimberly's medical chart, which he had brought with him. "Here is the sheet of symptoms that Dr. Ziegler told you about when we met yesterday." He gravely pointed out the more serious symptoms. "She may experience tiredness more easily, shortness of breath, a lack of appetite, or any of the rest of these symptoms. Keep a close eye on her. If you see any of them, please call your physician and come here immediately."

The solid, brawny man gave them all the assurance he could. "You have my promise that we will do all we can. We are only a phone call away. Please let us know if you need any help."

Chapter Eight

For three months, while Larry reluctantly returned to work, Betty stayed home with the children. The worried, nervous mother carefully monitored Kimberly's every move. Larry phoned home twice a day (and sometimes more) to make sure things at home were stable.

Kimberly seemed to remain the same except for her skin color. It became a deeper blue and then gradually changed to a deep purple. There was no doubt she was getting worse, but still none of the other symptoms the doctor had described appeared.

One night, while half sleeping, Betty heard Kim's soft, weak cry. She jumped out of bed and raced to the crying baby's room to see what was wrong. Afraid of what she might find, the nervous mother turned on the light and cautiously approached the crib.

Carefully looking the situation over, the shaking mother could not find any visible reason for the child's tears. The infant had eaten just an hour ago, and she was completely dry. So immediately the half-sleeping woman began to inspect each part of her daughter's small body. She had left the list of symptoms beside the baby's bed. The uneasy mother picked it up. Chills? No. Fever? No. One by one she eliminated each of the warning signs listed. Relieved that none of those were present, Betty took the warmly wrapped baby into her arms and cradled her close. What was making Kim cry? Maybe she just needed to be comforted. Tired as she was, Betty took Kimberly out to the living room to rock her. This did not seem to help. Next, she walked around, slightly bouncing her. Still the infant whimpered. No matter what she tried, it did not help.

Frustrated, the sleepy mom sat in the rocking chair exhausted. She laid the tiny child across her lap facedown, with her chest and belly hanging between her knees. Slowly she patted the infant on the back, trying to think of what else she could do. Almost asleep, Betty suddenly realized that the crying had stopped and Kimberly was fast asleep. Glad that the ordeal was over, the loving mother gently picked her baby up to put her back in bed. But the slight movement caused the baby to whimper and then break into a full cry.

Betty picked her daughter up and headed back to the rocking chair, rocking and patting, rocking and patting. When would it end? It continued all night and on into the next day. Finally Betty could take no more. What if she was missing something? What if one of the symptoms was present and she didn't even know it? Larry hadn't seen any of them either. The thought gnawed at her until she phoned Dr. Joe in desperation and asked if she could come in that afternoon.

"Betty, thank you for your confidence in me," Dr. Bernier told the worn-out mother. "You should really take Kim to a pediatrician—someone who knows more about medical treatment for children. There is one in town who is very good. His name is Dr. John Michaels. Take her there. We don't want to take any chances, in case it is something more serious. I'll call and let him know you are coming."

With Brent and Kimberly dressed in warm clothes, Betty left the house as soon as she could. When they arrived at the pediatrician's office, the nurse took them in right away. She had been the one who had talked to Dr. Joe when he called. She knew that this case might be very critical.

The pediatrician asked several questions as he thoroughly examined the crying infant. He poked and prodded around her abdomen, took her temperature, felt her pulse, and listened to her heart and lungs. After a few minutes, he turned to the waiting mother, while rubbing his hand over his chin. "Mrs. Vinton, Kim has a serious case of gas buildup. In a small child like Kim the pain can be rather intense, even enough to make her cry. When her belly hangs down between your legs, that takes the pressure off and makes the pain go away. Here is a prescription for some medication that should bring her quick relief. If nothing changes by tomorrow afternoon, give me a call." Betty wasn't convinced that he was sure about his diagnosis, but *he* was the doctor. She thanked him and went directly to the pharmacy.

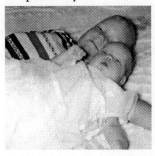

Immediately after arriving home, Brent went to his room to play, while Betty gave Kimberly her first dose of medication. The relief was not immediate, so Betty rocked and patted her precious daughter's back. Still there was no relief. A few hours later, when it was time for the next dose, the loving mother held her crying little girl in her arms and placed the small spoon in the baby's mouth. Still there was no relief. At the appropriate time, she gave another dose. Again there was no relief. After twenty-four hours all of the doses had been given, and the miserable baby was still crying. Betty took the pediatrician's advice, called him, and went to his office again. When the doctor saw the exhausted mother, he could tell she had not slept the night before.

The muscular, fair-skinned doctor looked Kimberly over again, shook his head, and bit his bottom lip in frustration. "Honestly, I don't know why that medication did not work. Perhaps, because of her heart defect, we should hospitalize her and monitor her overnight."

"I wish you would," Betty replied, relieved about getting help. "There is something wrong, but none of the symptoms from the list the cardiologist gave us are present."

The pediatrician stared at the floor in deep thought. "None of it makes sense," he said. "If it was her stomach, she would be better by now. But there are no other symptoms. With her heart problem, I don't want to take any chances. When you leave here, please go directly to the hospital. Since it is late in the day, I will meet you there."

Betty stopped by the front desk, called Larry, and left the office to go immediately to Midland Hospital. She could not help feeling shaken.

Getting into the car, Betty gave Brent strict instructions. "Brent," she said, "hold your sister and keep an eye on her. She has to go to the hospital as quickly as possible."

"All right, Mom. Is she okay?"

"I don't know."

By the time Betty arrived at the hospital with her children, her husband was already there. He and Dr. Michaels were anxiously awaiting their arrival in the busy emergency room lobby. Larry's presence brought Betty strength she wasn't sure she had. But her eyes became misty as they hugged. "Larry, what are we going to do?"

Larry responded by hugging her tightly, while grabbing Brent's small hand. "Jesus loves me this I know," he whispered in her ear.

Dr. Michaels took Kimberly from her mother. He wanted other doctors to assess her condition. Betty started to follow. "Betty, could you wait in the lobby, please?" Dr. Michaels said in a reassuring way. After we examine Kimberly and do a few tests, we will call you to the examination room."

"Okay," Betty replied, as she sat down next to Larry and Brent.

Larry put his arm around her shoulders. "I talked to your mother, and she and your dad are on their way here to get Brent. They said he can stay with them as long as we need."

With a look of relief, Betty leaned around Larry to talk to their son. "Grandma and Grandpa are coming to get you!" she told him.

"They are? Do I get to spend the night with them?" the young child shrieked. His eyes sparkled at the news.

"Yes, you do. We will call you tomorrow to check on you."

"Okay."

Guilt always took over both parents when they had to send Brent someplace so they could take care of Kim. Somehow God had kept the little boy from being affected by the time away from his parents. "Thank you, Lord!" the appreciative father whispered quietly.

After Brent left, Dr. Riley, the chief of pediatrics, came out to speak with the concerned parents. He hesitated, hoping for just the right words. "Kimberly seems to be in some sort of distress," Dr. Riley began. "Neither Dr. Michaels nor I can find the cause of her discomfort. We would like to keep her overnight for observation." Looking at Betty, he could tell she was very exhausted. "Mom," he continued, looking straight at Betty, "this will give you a chance to catch up on your sleep."

The tired mother nodded in agreement. "What is making Kim cry like that?" she asked, hoping for a definitive answer.

"At this point we just aren't sure. Crying is the only symptom we can find, so far. She seems so uncomfortable, and nothing we do helps her."

"Yes, I know exactly what you mean. She has been like that for two days now." Betty didn't realize how far forward she was slumping from exhaustion. "If she has to spend the night, can one of us stay with her?"

Dr. Riley shook his head. "No. I'm sorry. That is against hospital policy. All of the infants stay together in the nursery, and parents aren't allowed in that area."

"So you just want us to leave her in your hands in this condition?" Larry asked with a frown.

"Mr. and Mrs. Vinton, it would be good if you got as much sleep as you possibly can and returned in the morning. This will give us plenty of time to figure out what is going on. If there is any change, we will notify you immediately. I promise!" Dr. Riley tried hard to reassure the couple.

The car felt very empty as the parents made their way home.

Chapter Nine

Early the next morning, Betty rolled over in her bed dazed and confused. What was that noise? It sounded the same over and over again in her sleep. Now, partially awake, she realized...*the phone*! Jumping out of bed, she sprinted to the wall where the phone hung near the kitchen. "Hello?" She wondered who would be waking them up so early.

"Mrs. Vinton, this is Dr. Michaels. Mrs. Vinton? Are you there?"

"Yes, yes. What's the matter?"

"Mrs. Vinton," he said again. He could tell she had been sleeping and repeated her name to make sure she was focused.

"Yes."

"This is Dr. Michaels. Kimberly's condition seems to be declining. You and Mr. Vinton need to come immediately and pick her up. She needs to see Dr. Ziegler as quickly as possible. We have determined that she is crying because she is having some sort of chest pains related to her heart condition." Then the pediatrician went on to explain that a few of the symptoms they had all been watching for were beginning to appear.

"No!" Betty shouted as Larry came running to her side. "NO! She needs to gain more weight! That hospital is so far away. It takes nearly three hours to get there. Call an ambulance."

"Mrs. Vinton, please hurry! In the time it would take for us to arrange an ambulance, you could be halfway there. Please come, and hurry!"

"Okay. We'll come right away."

Larry could not figure out to whom his wife was talking and what was going on. His mind was still foggy from sleep. As Betty hung up the receiver, she turned to him while running down the hall. "Larry, Kim is getting worse. The doctors think that her crying is somehow related to her heart. They want us to come immediately and take her to Henry Ford Hospital. There isn't time to arrange an ambulance."

Both parents were shaking as they put themselves into "high gear." Dressing quickly, they were soon in the car and on their way. "I knew it!" Betty sobbed. "I should have gone with my motherly instinct and taken her to see her cardiologist yesterday. Now here we are, traveling that long distance in a state of emergency."

Larry held her hand while he drove toward the hospital. "There was no way you could have known. You did your best and followed the doctor's orders. Don't blame yourself. Let's just concentrate on getting her there quickly."

When the couple arrived at Midland Hospital, a nurse was standing at the front door waiting for them. She hurried the Vintons inside to check in with the doctor and pick up their daughter.

Dr. Michaels met briefly with the couple. He knew it was important that Kimberly be examined by her cardiologist. "I'll call the cardiologist and let him know that you are on the way. Don't stop! Time is of the essence."

Opening her door, Larry helped Betty into the car. With the baby cradled in her arms, Betty settled in as her husband took the driver's seat. As they drove out of the driveway, a sense of peace washed over them, even though they were not sure what was going to happen. "Jesus, our Savior, is with us," they reminded each other.

During the trip Larry drove well over the speed limit, hoping against hope that a policeman would pull them over and offer an even faster police escort. But no one stopped them the whole way. The focused father was able to knock an entire forty-five minutes off the journey.

In the meantime Betty tried to feed Kimberly so that she would not be hungry when they arrived. Betty did not have much success though, because the hurting child could not quit crying enough to eat.

In the emergency room, Kim's cardiologist and surgeon were anxiously anticipating the Vintons' arrival. Seeing the parents coming down the hall, the physicians met them halfway. "Mr. and Mrs. Vinton, it is good to see you both again," Dr. Ziegler said as he greeted them and shook their hands. "We are going to take Kim for some tests. We would like to meet you in my office on the thirteenth floor in an hour."

"Can't we go with her?" asked Betty.

"No, I'm sorry. It won't be more than an hour."

As promised, within an hour, Dr. Ziegler walked into his office, with Kimberly lying quietly in his arms. Betty quickly stood up to take her daughter.

"Kim's discomfort was definitely coming from her chest," the cardiologist said, looking at them both with strong, caring eyes. "She was given some medication to relieve the pressure she was feeling. Has she gained any weight since you were last here?"

"Not really," Betty responded. "She has gained barely a pound. She seems to eat less and less because it tires her so quickly."

Dr. Ziegler nodded his head in understanding. Tapping his pen against his fingers, he began, "We reviewed Kimberly's medical chart from her last visit and examined her carefully today." He paused to exhale a nervous cough. "My colleagues and I agree that Kimberly is at a point that she needs to have something done to help her. Her crying is the result of chest pain from small heart attacks."

Betty gasped slightly as she grimaced at the thought.

"She needs the surgery we talked about three months ago. We would like to give her a day to rest and then operate the day after tomorrow. The Blalock-Taussig shunt will provide the oxygen she needs. During this surgery the bodies of blue babies, such as Kim, absorb the extra oxygen immediately. When she comes out of surgery, she will be pinker than you have ever seen her."

The thrill of seeing the change washed over both mother and father. They gave each other a quick hug.

Dr. Ziegler let them revel in the warm feeling that the news had brought. He knew they would not react the same way to the other information he needed to share. "At the same time," he continued, "you should know that the risk is very, very high. Even though the surgery has been around a few years, the survival rate is in the low percentile. Kimberly's size and age will increase the risk."

"What kind of risk are we talking about, Doctor?" the father asked in an interrogating tone.

"She has less than a 10 percent chance to survive, but without it she has none."

The parents looked at each other with moisture collecting in their eyes. There was really no choice about what to do. In one way that made it easier to send her to surgery. On the other hand, they knew the possibility of losing their daughter was very real.

Larry and Betty wiped their cheeks. Then Larry inquired, "Could we please have a few minutes to think things through?"

"Sure." The cardiologist understood their position. "Why don't I leave you alone and come back in a few minutes?"

The parents held each other as they were absorbed in their private thoughts. After a few minutes, Larry gently pushed Betty back to look into her eyes. "We have to be confident in our Lord, Betty. He has led us to this place at this time for a reason. He is with us always and will be with Kim too. We should go forward with the surgery."

Shaking and sobbing, Betty shook her head in agreement. It would not be easy to watch her daughter go through so much pain, but the devoted mother knew this was the only option for her baby to have a chance at life. Jesus was in charge. They must place their confidence in him.

A couple minutes later, the cardiologist returned with the surgeon, who offered to answer any questions the parents might have.

"No questions," Larry responded. "We are certain the surgery is the only option. Please take good care of our baby."

As the surgeon shook the parents' hands to confirm to them that he would do everything he could to help Kimberly, Larry noticed for the first time how large the surgeon's hands were. He gave Betty a sideways glance to see if she noticed too.

Two days later, on October 15, 1960, the Vinton's closest family members and their pastor gathered in Kimberly's small hospital room, waiting for the nurse to take her to surgery. Each person had come to bring comfort and strength. They were all comforted by the fact that they could be together.

At 7:50 AM the nurse slipped into the room to announce that the surgical team was almost ready. Someone from the operating team would come to get Kimberly in approximately ten minutes. One by one the grandparents supportively moved close to Betty, Larry, and Kimberly, each wanting his or her own moment to hug, kiss, and talk to the dark purple infant.

After everyone had a chance to be seated again, Pastor Martin asked for silence, as he moved to the seat next to the crying mother. With his right hand over the baby's heart, he gave her a special blessing and began, "Let us pray." All immediately bowed their heads. "Dear heavenly Father, we come to thy throne of grace today on behalf of thy dear, small child, Kimberly. Bless her as she undergoes this most delicate surgery. Guide the hands of the surgeons by thy holy power. Help the whole surgical team do their jobs to the best of their abilities. Thank you for the faith thou hast placed in Kimberly through thy Word and her baptism. Knowing that she is a child of God, we have the comfort that thou art with her. We ask that this precious little one may be brought back to us in better health, having been healed by thy divine power. We know that thou workest all things together for good and according to thy holy will. Therefore, we commend her to thy care, knowing that whatever future thou hast for her will be for thy glory alone. We also ask that thou wouldst be with Larry and Betty and all of us who wait here during the surgery. Please take away our anxieties and replace them with a confidence in thy holy will. We ask this in Jesus' name as we pray together.

Our Father, who art in heaven, hallowed be thy name, thy kingdom come, thy will be done on earth as it is in heaven. Give us this day our daily bread; and forgive us our trespasses, as we forgive those who trespass against us; and lead us not into temptation, but deliver us from evil. For thine is the kingdom and the power and the glory forever and ever. Amen."

Betty rocked Kimberly and wept silently.

As the pastor concluded his prayer, a tall, slender, smiling nurse returned and asked Betty and Larry to follow her with Kimberly. "This is against standard procedure," she told them, "but this surgery is such a high risk that your cardiologist has requested that you be allowed to carry Kimberly to the corridor just outside the operating room doors."

The parents stood to follow the neatly dressed nurse, each giving the other a nervous, pleading look. This was the moment they had sadly anticipated; every second they had with their baby girl was precious.

The nurse led them down a long hallway to the door where they would leave Kimberly in the hands of the capable surgical team. "When you are ready," she explained, "knock on the door to let the technician know you are ready."

"Okay. Thank you." Both parents replied appreciatively.

The silent, struggling parents hung onto their baby as long as they thought they could, tears flowing freely. They knew this surgery was the best answer. At the same time, not knowing the outcome made them treasure their last few minutes even more. After standing close together holding the baby and each other, each parent gave her one last long hug and several kisses. "We love you, sweetheart! We love you so much! Jesus is with you!" With that, they knocked on the door, and a surgical assistant came to take Kimberly. Slowly the mother and father reluctantly placed their baby into his arms, and the father placed one final kiss on her forehead.

As soon as the baby arrived in the operating room, the surgeon, his assistant, an anesthetist, a graduate nurse, and a student nurse gathered around the small purple body. They all looked nervously at one another to assure themselves that everyone was ready. The surgeon addressed all of them. "As we discussed in our meeting this morning, this surgery will be especially intricate. Until further notice there will be no more unnecessary talking or movement. You all are very good at the jobs you do. Your best work is essential. This baby is very small." The surgeon always made it a practice to give his staff a short pep talk to encourage them to do their best.

"Before we begin, please chart all stats: blood pressure, heart rate, temperature, everything. If there is a change at any time, please call out my name and what has changed." This was standard procedure for every surgery, but in this case miscommunication could cost the life of a baby. He gave them a few moments to make sure everything was in order.

"Now, if everyone is ready, we will begin." Knowing that there was additional surgery in the future for this little girl, the doctor was very specific about where the incision needed to be placed. This baby girl would someday become a woman. He didn't want the incision to interfere with that development. Slowly and precisely he followed the lines he had drawn on her chest earlier. Blood oozed from the site. The suction tool was immediately in place. If only the rest of the surgery would be this easy.

Chapter Ten

After Betty and Larry returned to Kimberly's room, a nurse asked the group to go to the surgical waiting room down the hall. The room had refreshments available as well as reading material to keep the waiting family occupied. This group thought visiting and drinking coffee was a great way to help the tense parents pass the time. It did in one way, but still each moment seemed like an eternity.

While the waiting friends and family socialized, the nurse came intermittently to report on each surgical milestone. First she came to let them know that Kimberly had been hooked up to the necessary equipment successfully and without incident.

A half hour later she stopped by to announce that the surgery had begun.

Forty-five minutes after that, the large, round woman reported that Kimberly's blood pressure had dropped significantly at one point but was quickly brought under control by placing a clamp on a certain artery for a short amount of time.

No one came to say anything for quite awhile. The parents began to worry. Why hadn't anyone come to make an announcement in the last hour? Was there another complication?

Finally, the surgical assistant came through the door. He sat down next to Betty, not really showing any sign of what kind of news he was bringing. Betty's heart sank. Larry put his arm around her. Tears decorated the corners of each of their eyes.

"The operation is over," he began. "We haven't done many of these Blalock-Taussig shunts at this hospital. Watching always gives me goose bumps. The doctor connected the arteries, took off all of the clamps, and in a heartbeat Kimberly's color turned from dark purple to a beautiful pink. It was the most wonderful sight to behold!" The assistant looked off into the distance, as if reliving the very moment they had seen one heartbeat change this little baby's life. He willed himself into the present, looking at each parent with pride and satisfaction. "It was like seeing a miracle right before my very own eyes! The surgeon will be in soon to share the details with you."

Explosions of joy and appreciation rippled across the room. Larry thanked the man who had been second in command in the operating room. "You'll probably never know how much we appreciate all you have done," Larry began. "Please thank the entire surgical team for us." The assistant left, agreeing to give the message to the rest of the team.

Long, tight hugs were exchanged among family and friends. The pastor once again asked for silence. "Let us pray. Dear gracious, heavenly Father, thank you for hearing and granting our requests concerning Kimberly. Because of your abiding love, we were willing to accept thy will. Thou hast chosen to leave thy little lamb here on earth. Thank you. Thank you for being with the surgeon and his helpers. Please remain with us all as we care for this child of thine during her recuperation. If it is thy will, please allow the Vintons to return home soon to their son, Brent, who also needs their attention. Also be with him and keep him from all harm and danger until his family returns home. We ask this in Jesus' holy and precious name. Amen."

By the time everyone got control of their emotions, Dr. Lam walked in with a revealing smile on his face. He reached out to shake the hands of both parents and sat on the arm of the soft blue couch. "Betty, Larry," he began, nodding to the excited parents, while seemingly in deep thought, "you are Christians, aren't you?"

Betty and Larry looked at him quizzically. "Yes, why?" Larry responded.

"I can always tell when I am operating on a child from a Christian family. I don't know what it is, but a sense of calm and determination sets in."

The anxious parents smiled back at him, still anticipating his review of Kim's operation.

"Kim came through the surgery with flying colors, the main color being pink. We rerouted and connected the vein, and in a heartbeat she turned pink. I can't wait for you to see her.

"The next forty-eight hours are the most crucial. Kimberly will need to be watched every minute for about a week. We have arranged for a private nurse to sit with her around the clock during that period." The doctor watched the parents' reaction. They were eager to support his decisions any way they could. He continued. "She is still connected to tubes and wires, but if you can handle that, you may see her when you're ready."

"Can we go *now?*" the thrilled, animated father asked.

With a little chuckle, the doctor nodded his head. "Everyone can come, but only for a few minutes. She will be behind glass to protect her from germs."

All seven people gathered their belongings and made their way down the hall with the doctor. As they approached the glassed-in area where Kim was lying, the doctor turned to remind them about the wires and tubes. The group remembered his earlier words.

A gasp came from almost everyone in the small crowd. Betty was in the first row and could not believe her eyes. "Look! She's pink! Look! She's pink! Larry, Larry, she's pink!"

Larry came to stand beside her, almost leaning on the glass to make sure what he thought he saw was actually there. "Betty, look at her fingers and toes. They are all pink!" Betty nodded but could not keep her eyes from staring at the bottoms of Kimberly's feet.

"They're bright pink," she shared in total amazement. "They're very, very pink! No more purple." The thankful mother could only stare at her daughter and let her eyes leak the teardrops. "Pink. Amazing!"

After a few more hugs, the friends and relatives walked back to the waiting room and gave the parents some time alone. But as they parted ways, Betty heard her mother-in-law speak to her husband. "Honey, can we please go find a blue dress for Kim? She can finally wear blue. She just has to have a blue dress!" The grandfather grinned and took his wife shopping.

A short time later, the cardiologist came by to check Kimberly. Betty and Larry were still staring through the glass when Dr. Ziegler entered the recovery area. They were having trouble leaving their daughter in the care of the nurses. The doctor pointed to her pink fingers and toes with a broad smile on his face. Both parents acknowledged his enthusiasm by moving their heads up and down. "Thank you so much," they mouthed.

Dr. Ziegler came out of the infant's room. "You are so welcome." The doctor was always appreciative of thanks and encouragement. "Dr. Bernier called to find out how Kim is doing. I explained that the surgery went smoothly and that her improvement is already visible. He wanted you to know that he is thinking about you and that Larry's Aunt Florine is coming tomorrow morning to help out while Kim needs special care. Nurses are very expensive, and she wanted to do something to help."

"That's my aunt," Larry informed the doctor. "She is the one who noticed that Kim's skin color was not right. She is so sweet!"

The cardiologist nodded and continued talking to the couple for quite some time, explaining what would take place over the next few days. "If Kimberly continues to improve, they will slowly begin weaning her from all the tubes in two days. On the third day, they will feed her by mouth, so the intravenous nutrients can be discontinued." Then the doctor showed them a list of things that would take place each day.

"When this list of items has been accomplished, she should be allowed to go home," he continued. The doctor did not want to appear overconfident. At the same time, Betty and Larry needed to know the plan he was laying out so they could see the light at the end of the tunnel.

"Do you have any questions?" he asked.

The motherly instinct in Betty came rushing out. "When can I hold her? How often will we be allowed to visit?"

"You will probably be able to touch her tomorrow. Touching should be minimal to prevent infection. It is important that she be touched and talked to by her parents, but please be careful. The nurses will regulate how often you can visit and the length of time you can stay. It will all depend on Kim's well-being."

The elated mom and dad shook hands with the cardiologist as he departed. "Again, thank you, so much!" Larry reiterated.

With Aunt Florine by her side and everyone concentrating their efforts on whatever they could do to help, Kimberly recovered very quickly. Within a week the active baby no longer needed a special nurse. Florine was thankful, as sitting those long hours and watching her young niece go through so much distressed her. She was glad to be there to help, but she would be glad when it was over. Betty and Larry were grateful for her role in Kim's quick recovery.

Kimberly was released from the hospital after only ten days. Before the small family left, the cardiologist asked them to stop by his office to review a list of "do's" and "don'ts" concerning the baby's care at home. "Your follow-up visit is scheduled for two weeks from Thursday," the doctor said in conclusion. "Do either of you have any questions?"

Betty did. "Now that we have crossed this swaying bridge, what should we expect for the future?"

"Well," the doctor said hesitantly, "this is one of those situations where we don't have any statistics. Most babies born with this defect do not survive, so there is little information on which to base a long-term evaluation.

"Kimberly *will* need more surgery in the future. When? Nobody knows. There is no way to tell. Frankly, we didn't expect her to live long enough to have this surgery, let alone survive it. Now, look at her. She is pink and energetic.

"Another operation will be necessary as her body grows and needs more oxygen. Dr. Lam and I predict it will be in the next couple years. Let's take one step at a time. She will need to come back one month after her two-week visit. After that, every three months should be sufficient for a while."

"Does she have any restrictions?"

"There won't be any that you need to worry about. As she grows, she will limit herself according to how much energy she has. Treat her the same way you treat her brother."

The satisfied couple thanked the doctor for all he had done. Having already packed their things, they were on their way home in no time.

Chapter Eleven

Everyone in the Vinton family of four was glad to be back together. It was hard to believe they had been home for a week already. Betty was especially glad to be in her usual routine. Larry had returned to work the Monday after they had come home. Kimberly was making headway to being totally healed, and Brent did not appear to have any ill effects from having spent so much time away from his family. He doted over his baby sister every chance he got. The caring, happy youngster was a great help to his mother.

As Kimberly grew, Betty and either Larry or Ann, one of Betty's dearest friends, took her to the cardiologist on a regular basis. Between visits the mother and father watched their daughter carefully for any signs of change in her physical ability, stamina, and color. Because of her condition, Kimberly wasn't able to keep up with the other children in the neighborhood, but it never seemed to bother her. The fact that her loving brother always waited for her to catch up helped tremendously.

One day, as Betty was standing in the living room watching her children play in the yard, she noticed Kim sitting on the porch in her rocking chair. Opening the front door, the concerned mother stepped out to see how she was feeling. As her daughter turned her head to look up, Betty noticed she seemed more tired than usual.

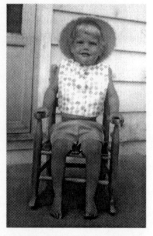

Betty sat down beside her almost four-year-old miracle child and stretched out her legs. As she did so, the curious mother noticed that Kimberly's lips had a slight hint of blue to them. Perplexed, the mother leaned over to give her daughter a hug. "Are you feeling okay?"

The little girl looked her mother in the face and replied. "Yes. I can't play tag, so I'm just watching."

"Why can't you play?" the frowning mother asked.

"I just get too tired," her daughter answered.

"Oh." The mother shook her head and placed a kiss on the child's forehead. She lifted the little girl's hand into her own. Sure enough, the blueness was coming back into her nails, both on her fingers and on her toes. It was time for them to make another trip to the cardiologist.

Since it was only January, Dr. Ziegler was surprised to see Kimberly and her mother again so soon. Hadn't it been just a few months since their last visit? "How are things going at home, Mom?" he addressed Betty curiously.

"Kim seems to be losing some of her energy and stamina. Her color is not as pink as it used to be. She also rests more often. We thought it would be a good idea to have her evaluated."

"How old is she now?" the doctor inquired.

"She turned four last month," the mother informed him.

"Well, let's take a look. Kimberly, can you hop up onto the table so I can listen to your heart and lungs?" The cardiologist immediately helped the little girl jump to her destination.

Kim lay back on the examination table slowly, anticipating the cold touch of the stethoscope against her skin. First, the doctor felt the pounding of her heart with his palm. Next, he placed his stethoscope in his hand to warm it before placing it on her chest. Positioning the medical device just over her ribs, he listened carefully. Then he slowly turned to her eagerly waiting mother. "The shunt still sounds as though it is working to its full potential," he commented excitedly.

Having heard everything he had anticipated, Dr. Ziegler had Kim roll over on her back. He listened to her lungs. He let another grin slip from his lips. "Her lungs are clear too."

After spending a few moments rereading Kimberly's medical chart and making notations on it, the physician rotated himself in his chair to face Betty. "Kim's heart and lungs all sound good. After looking back and studying her medical history, I am thinking that perhaps she is approaching the time for her second surgery.

"Maybe you could document her health progression on a weekly basis. When you come back next month, we will compare notes."

Betty nodded in affirmation, tears forming in her eyes. On the one hand, she was thankful that the cardiologist was honest and up-front, but then again, thinking about a second surgery for Kim made her heart break.

During the long drive home, Betty wondered how she would tell her husband what Dr. Ziegler had said. How and when was she going to tell him that his baby girl needed more surgery? By the time Betty got home from the visit to the cardiologist, Larry was in bed. Betty tucked her sleeping child into her bed and then tiptoed into her own room. Larry was sound asleep. She felt bad for him because he could not go with her that day. But now, how was she going to tell him? While she changed into her nightgown, her conversation with the cardiologist played out in her mind.

"Have you noticed any changes in Kimberly's health?" Dr. Ziegler had asked.

"Yes, she can only walk two or three steps before she needs to squat and breathe. Her lips are so purple that people constantly ask if she has been eating grape popsicles. I don't know if this is relevant or not, but the other night our family was sitting and watching TV when we noticed that Kim was chewing on something. She had stored food from dinner up in her cheeks. Isn't that odd?" She had tried to carefully describe Kimberly's health.

Dr. Ziegler had thought briefly and then responded. "She probably gets too tired from chewing her food at the table. She stores it for later. She probably doesn't even realize she is doing it. Her oxygen saturation has declined to an all-time low. We should seriously consider doing the second surgery. It will be the same as the first one, only we will use a vein from her right arm instead of her left."

She had answered, "That is the news I was expecting to hear, but how will I tell my husband?"

The disturbed mother finished getting ready for bed. Should she wake Larry up or wait and tell him in the morning? He really needed a good night's sleep. As these thoughts flitted through her head, she accidentally knocked something off the dresser. Larry was awake instantly and sat up in bed. "I'm glad you're back safe and sound," he said through his fogged mind. Then he realized that Betty must have news from the cardiologist. "What did Dr. Ziegler have to say?"

His wife sadly looked him in the eyes. Then her emotions took over. She reached for his hand. "Oh, Larry, Kim needs more surgery. Dr. Ziegler said we need to do it soon."

Larry stared at her while the information sank in. "No! They are not going to cut on my daughter again! They can't!" Then sob after sob was released from his innermost being.

Betty began to cry aloud. She touched her sorrowing husband on the arm. "Larry, this is not what we wanted to hear. But Dr. Ziegler was very adamant that we should give it serious consideration. He went ahead and scheduled her for surgery on January 13. He wants us to bring her back next month so he can run the tests again. If her health has declined in any way, he wants to go through with the surgery."

Larry continued to weep. "We won't. They are not going to cut on her anymore."

Betty didn't know what to say. "Larry, soon it will be a matter of life or death. Wouldn't it be better to do it while she has a better chance for survival? Jesus is with us always. Remember?"

Larry kissed his wife, gave her a hug, and fell asleep thinking about her words.

Chapter Twelve

The day of surgery, January 13, 1965, was a cold, blustery day. The Vintons gathered together with their pastor and family in the surgical waiting room. Kimberly's second Blalock-Taussig shunt procedure was scheduled to begin in an hour. Everyone listened intently as Pastor Martin began the morning with a special devotion on the tenth chapter of John, verses 27 and 28. He read, "My sheep hear my voice, and I know them, and they follow me: and I give unto them eternal life; and they shall never perish, neither shall any man pluck them out of my hand."

In detail the thoughtful pastor reminded each person how God cares for them each and every day. "Just like a shepherd, he watches our every move, sends his angels to be by our sides for protection, and will not let us stray out of his hands. Those same hands were nailed to the cross so that when we fall into sin like lost, wandering sheep, we can claim everlasting life for Jesus' sake. John 3:16 reminds us that the love he has for us is the greatest love there is: 'For God so loved the world, that he gave his only begotten Son, that whosoever believeth in him should not perish, but have everlasting life.' This eternal life in heaven is for *all* who believe in Jesus Christ as their Savior. That includes children and adults." Pastor Martin then handed out the hymn sheets he had copied and brought with him. "Let's begin on the second page." The group broke out in one of Kim's favorite hymns, "I Am Jesus' Little Lamb."

> I am Jesus' little lamb;
> Ever glad at heart I am,
> For my Shepherd gently guides me,
> Knows my need and well provides me,
> Loves me ev'ry day the same,
> Even calls me by my name.
>
> Day by day, at home, away,
> Jesus is my Staff and Stay.

When I hunger, Jesus feeds me,
Into pleasant pastures leads me;
When I thirst, he bids me go
Where the quiet waters flow.

Who so happy as I am,
Even now the Shepherd's lamb?
And when my short life is ended,
By his angel hosts attended,
He shall fold me to his breast,
There within his arms to rest. Amen.

"Let us pray," the pastor concluded. "Dear gracious heavenly Father, we bring to thy throne of grace one of the sheep from thy fold. As our Good Shepherd, please bless Kimberly and all who are attending to her. Guide the surgeon's hands that his work may be done skillfully and quickly. Bless all the nurses and assistants, giving them an extra measure of understanding, knowledge, and confidence. As the Great Physician, Lord, we especially ask thee to guard, bless, and keep Kim in thy loving care, that she may live to thy glory forever. Grant her swift healing and a speedy recovery. Most of all, Lord, remind her and us that thou art our only Lord and Savior, our Good Shepherd, and that thou wilst guide all things according to thy holy will! Grant us all comfort, patience, and understanding in all things. We ask this in Jesus our Savior's name. Amen."

"Amen" echoed around the room as the prayer concluded.

The minister left his seat to place the sign of the cross on Kimberly's heart and forehead, imparting to her a special blessing. "May the Lord be with you, Kimberly Jean Vinton." Eight minutes later a nurse came to take the young, purple child to surgery.

Like last time, the nurse made announcements about the progression of the surgery. After the family's long, slow wait of three and a half hours, the surgeon entered the room. Betty feared the look she saw on his face. He was concentrating too hard to be bringing good news. Her mind raced. What would he have to say? But just as quickly as the thoughts appeared, they disappeared, as the stout man with large hands looked up at both parents. Taking off his glasses to wipe his face, he broke into a half-cocked smile and gave them each a nod. "The surgery was successful! Kimberly is as pink as can be!" A tear glistened in his eye. His heart was compassionate for children with bad hearts.

After the relieved parents and their family absorbed the news, Betty could not stop herself from leaning over and giving Dr. Lam the biggest hug he had ever experienced. "Thank you! Thank you!"

The surgeon continued. "The thanks should go to the whole surgical team. They were all well-prepared and delivered accurate, expedient work."

"Please tell them thank you for us," Larry requested.

Dr. Lam nodded with pride. "I sure will, from all three of us!"

"The nurses are finishing up the postoperative procedures. When they are done, they will let you know where to go to see Kim. She'll remain in intensive care for three or four days. Then she will be moved to a regular room. If she recovers as quickly as she did last time, she should be able to go home in about a week to ten days."

That statement brought a smile to Larry's and Betty's lips. As the physician rose to leave, he looked into the grateful parents' eyes. "She is one blessed little girl," he said.

Everyone in the waiting group looked at each other before joyfully bursting into a hymn of praise, led by Pastor Martin. "Praise God, from whom all blessings flow; praise him, all creatures here below; praise him above, ye heavenly hosts; praise Father, Son, and Holy Ghost." This song was followed by a short prayer. Betty and Larry thanked everyone, especially the pastor. He had been so faithful about encouraging them with God's Word.

Betty and Larry spent every day with Kim, sitting by her side, trying to keep her body quiet and her mind occupied. The job was rather easy, as her energy level was low. She enjoyed playing quiet board games.

On the third morning of recovery, the rested, refreshed parents arrived at the hospital to visit their daughter. They had decided to come a little early, since they were up and ready. After passing the nurses' station, they arrived at room 302. Betty slowly peeked around the corner into her daughter's room, hoping to see her sitting up a little or showing some sign of progress. As her eyes focused in on Kim's bed, fear and terror pierced her heart. Kimberly's bed was empty and had been made up with fresh sheets. Shock coursed through her body, and she began to shake. Without taking time to tell Larry what she had seen, she ran to the nurses' station. "Where is my daughter? Where is she? You didn't call us or anything!" Larry followed closely behind, the worst of fears running through his mind.

One of the nurses vaulted from behind the desk. "Oh, Mrs. Vinton! Come with me." The short brunette hurried her to a small room at the end of the hall. "Please come right in here," the nurse instructed, pointing to a small waiting area. "There is an explanation!"

The crying mother and disturbed father rushed to keep up with the hospital worker. As they anticipated what explanation there could be, they rounded the corner to the small lobby-like room. And there, sitting in the middle of the floor, was Kimberly, pink as could be, playing a game with one of the other patients. She got up and ran to see her mom and dad as they entered.

"This is our playroom," the calm, smiling nurse explained. "As soon as children feel well enough after surgery, they are allowed to come down here to play. Being active helps these patients heal more quickly. Your daughter woke up this morning ready to play. We were surprised, but we didn't want to hold her back."

Betty took in a deep breath, sighed, and began wiping the tears that flooded her face. "You have no idea how scary it was to find an empty, freshly sheeted bed. Intellectually I knew you would call if you needed us for any reason, but my emotions overrode my intellect. Thank you so much." The relieved mother leaned over to hug the nurse.

"I'm sorry too. I tried to keep this from happening by watching for you. Somehow I missed you," the nurse apologized as she left the room to finish the task she had been working on.

The rest of Kimberly's recovery was speedy. On the eighth day of her hospital stay, her cardiologist stopped by for one last visit. "Today's the day!" he told the parents with full enthusiasm. "Are you ready to take her home?"

"Yes," the newly energized yet nervous couple responded as they shook their heads.

"Over the last few days, we have tried to teach you everything about caring for Kim at home. It's most important that you care for her like a normal child. Don't give her any special privileges. Treat her just like you do her brother. She has a heart condition, but if you protect and smother her, you will turn her into an invalid."

"Okay," the parents said storing the advice in the back of their minds. "Thank you for everything."

A humble smile tugged at the corner of the cardiologist's mouth. "You're very welcome. Please keep in mind that this surgery is not a total correction. Your little girl's heart still has only one working ventricle, but when you get home she will have new-found energy.

"You should probably come back in about three weeks. We should monitor her every month for the next three months. If her health stays as good as it is now, she can come once a year after that."

As the physician and Larry shook hands, Betty got her daughter ready for the drive home.

Chapter Thirteen

The routine at the Vinton's home returned to normal more quickly than it had after Kim's first surgery. Brent was having the time of his life in second grade. Larry returned to his job as an engineer at Dow Chemical Company. Betty stayed home with Kim, who was appreciating her full bundle of get-up-and-go. For the first time, the chubby, happy little girl was doing things that she had not had the health to do before, things like getting into the cupboards to pull out pots and pans, pulling out all of the toys in her toy box, and running in the yard. The doctor had prepared Betty for this. He had told her that children sometimes regress to activities that they had never experienced.

As the watchful mother saw Kimberly pulling the pots and pans out of the cupboard, she thought about how her son had done these things when he was only one. She was so excited to watch her daughter pull toys out of her toy box and spread them all over the room. What a wondrous activity level her daughter had acquired—activity after activity without any squatting to rest!

Betty watched these activities for several weeks with pride and thankfulness until one day, when she heard a strange noise coming from Brent's bedroom. He was at school that day. What could possibly be going on? She stepped into the room to look around, and there, hanging from the curtains, was Kimberly, swinging as high as she could. The drapes were barely hanging onto their rods. All of a sudden, as if she had been slapped across the face, Betty realized what had been happening. She had been so caught up in watching Kim's new energy level that she had allowed the little stinker to do anything and everything she wanted without any limitations or responsibilities.

Dr. Ziegler's voice rang in her ears: "Treat her like you treat your son." The amused but stern mother should have known what was happening. Wasn't it just this morning that she had asked Kim to pick up her toys? Hadn't the mischievous little girl immediately squatted, started breathing hard, and looked into her mother's eyes pleadingly, saying, "I can't, Mama; it makes me too tired!"? Betty had caught onto that trick but had let it go. Hmm! Things definitely had to change.

After putting things into perspective, Betty immediately followed the suggestion of the doctor. She snatched Kimberly up, spanked her on the rear, and sat her on the couch. The cardiologist had told the young mother that it was okay to punish Kim as she would her other child. "She will turn blue from crying," Betty remembered him saying, "but sit her on the couch until she stops crying and turns pink." That is exactly what she did.

During the next visit to the cardiologist, Betty thanked him for his advice. After telling him the "curtain" story, she giggled mildly. "Your words came to mind that day when I realized her behavior was out of control. It took us both a few days to adjust to the new rules, but all is well now."

The cardiologist chuckled. He had been examining Kim as Betty told the story. "Thank you," he said, with an amused grin on his face. After telling the five-year-old little girl she could get dressed, the doctor sat down at his desk to talk to her mother.

"Her heart sounds great, her lungs are clear, and her color is good," the doctor reported, rubbing his eyes and watching for the mother's reaction. "You don't need to come back for a full year."

Betty accepted his words with joy. "That's great! My husband and I agreed that when Kim got well enough to come once a year, we would think about having another child. He'll be so excited."

The physician leaned back in his chair with his hands behind his head, his white cotton coat hanging from his legs and his foot propped up on his filing cabinet drawer. He wanted this conversation to be informal, as if they were visiting over coffee. "Let's talk about the issues Kim will face in the future. As far as her heart condition goes, she should not need any more surgery until she is, at the least, twelve years old, unless she has any health problems. Of course, that will be a few years from now, during which time the medical world will learn more and more about congenital heart defects and their impacts.

"I keep thinking how nice it would be if we could just put some sort of wall between the ventricles of children like Kim. But how would a person put a wall in something as fragile as an egg? It's impossible. What we hope is that as time goes by there will be more and more information and experience so that by the time she is ready for her next surgery, hopefully, we'll know more about what to do for her."

Kim was now dressed and came to sit next to her mother. She sat quietly, swinging her legs, while watching both adults as they spoke to one another. Betty listened intensely to Dr. Ziegler and thought about what Kim's life might be like through the years. "What should we be doing with her in the meantime?" she asked.

"Well, it is just like last time. Treat her like you do her brother. Do not limit her activities. Her body will do that by itself. If an activity is too strenuous for her, she won't participate automatically without being told." The doctor stopped talking, stood up to adjust his belt, and sat back down.

"The medical staff at this hospital is very conscientious about educating parents. With every visit you will learn more and more information that will be important for you to know. As you learn, teach Kim. She should be able to care for herself when she becomes an adult. All moms and dads want their chronically ill children to have lives as normal as possible, but many parents, especially mothers, get so involved in their children's conditions that they have trouble letting go when it is time. Do you remember looking forward to becoming an independent adult? Did you look forward to taking care of yourself? Kim will naturally want to do the same thing. She should be supplied with everything she needs to be able to do that. Your daughter has a bright future ahead of her. We want her to be able to make the most of it. Besides that, you may not always be around to help her."

The proud mother was in full agreement with the cardiologist. Some day her daughter would want to move out or get married. She needed to know how to do that, and her mother had to cut the apron strings slowly, so she would not be clinging to her in fear of something going wrong.

The doctor shifted in his chair and pushed his glasses up on his nose. Betty felt good about the doctor's positive attitude and encouragement. Dr. Ziegler broke into her thoughts. "Because of the type of heart defect Kim has, there is quite a bit of pressure in her arteries. Cardiologists are recommending that children with heart defects not bear children. Between the lack of oxygen and the high blood pressure on her heart and lungs, the lives of the mother and baby would be at stake."

Betty blinked and stared at the doctor. What was he telling her? Her daughter could not have children? Growing up, getting married, and having children were every little girl's dream. She frowned and leaned forward in her seat, trying to make the doctor realize what he had just said. "Did you say no children?"

The cardiologist positioned himself so he could look the somewhat stunned mother in the eyes. First he called her by name. Her head moved toward him. "I did not say Kimberly could not have children. I said she should not *give birth* to children. Adoption is a very precious means God uses to get the right children to the right families. It is a wonderful fact of life."

"And how does a mother go about telling her daughter that type of information?" she said, thinking that there was no easy way to break such news.

"The same way you have told her everything else. As I have worked with you and Larry, the fact that you are always open and honest with Kim has been impressive. You keep her from having to sit and wonder what is going to happen next. You tell her everything you know right away so that there are no medical surprises pulled on her. That is very important to the psychological well-being of children. They never have to sit and wonder or worry. The same applies here. Not giving birth will be as natural to her as you make it. Since you are dedicated to keeping her informed, insert it into daily conversations. You don't have to dwell on it, but talk about it as easily as you do about her heart defect. It is just a part of her life."

Betty nodded her head. "That makes sense, I guess. It is somewhat of a shock to me, and I have never considered it that way. You're right. Adoption is wonderful. I have cousins who are adopted, but I never thought of it that way. My husband was adopted by his father, and that definitely has been a blessing to all of us. Thanks for presenting it that way."

While the Vinton family was eating dinner one evening, Betty was acting a little peculiar. Larry couldn't quite put his finger on what it was, but his wife was up to something, and he was going to find out what it was. They were eating cake for dessert when his suspicions got the best of him. "Betty, what are you holding back from me? You are acting a little giddy for this time of the day. Is everything okay? Is there something you need to tell me?"

Betty couldn't keep her secret any longer. "We're going to have a baby!" she announced to Larry and Brent and Kim.

Larry dropped his fork and took hold of her hand, pulling her so he could kiss her across the table. "That's great! Have you been to the doctor?"

"Yes," she answered, "I needed him to confirm what I had already surmised before I shared the news with you."

Both father and mother leaned over the chairs of their two children. The family enjoyed one big group hug!

Betty decided that her pregnancy was a great avenue for talking to Kim about having babies. She took some time to think through her approach of explaining that babies grow in their mommies' tummies. One little comment after the other flowed freely between the mother and daughter. Betty took some time to sit and talk directly to her daughter about her heart defect and about adoption. Kimberly listened intently. When her mother was finished, the tall, tender-hearted five-year-old little girl placed her arms lovingly around her mother's neck. She looked into her eyes. "I know, Mommy. The doctor already told us. Jesus has a special little girl picked out for me already."

Betty's heart was overwhelmed with surprise, relief, and gladness. She had no idea that Kim had been listening that day at the doctor's office. Adoption was already a natural topic to her daughter.

Chapter Fourteen

Loading the truck with all of their earthly possessions, Betty and Larry were confident about their decision. They were moving to Detroit so that Larry could attend the seminary to become a pastor. The Holy Spirit had worked in his heart the truths of God's Word and the desire to go and tell others about sin and God's forgiveness through Jesus Christ, their Savior.

Larry had had this desire for quite awhile, and now God had worked all things to his glory in perfect timing. Brent was entering sixth grade, Kim's health had stabilized, and even though Shaun Renae had been born six weeks early, she was two years old and growing fast. Added to those blessings were the facts that the seminary was on the same campus as the Christian day school for the children, the Vinton's house was located across the street from the campus, and they would be only six miles from Henry Ford Hospital, where Kim had had her two heart surgeries. Yes, this move was definitely God's will.

As the last item was put in the U-Haul, the neighbors came over to say goodbye. Hugs were given all around. A few tears were shed. No matter how excited the Vintons were about their new endeavor, they were going to miss their family, their friends, and living in this small town.

Getting settled into their new home did not take long. By the end of summer, the boxes were all unpacked, the children had made new friends with the neighborhood children, and Kim and Brent were attending the parochial school.

As the school year passed, Betty and Larry were happy to see their children enjoying their new surroundings. Brent was involved in school activities such as the choir, softball, and the operetta performance that the seventh through twelfth grade put on at the end of each school year. Kim took piano lessons, enjoyed being part of the children's choir, and even attempted to learn ballet, which turned out to be too much physical exertion for her. All the while, Shaun stayed home with her mother and "helped" around the house.

One afternoon Betty was in her usual cooking and house cleaning routine when she was interrupted by the telephone. It was Larry calling from the school. He explained that Kim was not feeling well and needed to come home from school. Just then Betty heard the doorbell. She opened the door and looked down. There stood Kim. "What's the matter, Honey?" she asked her daughter, helping her into the house.

"I don't feel good, Mama."

Guiding Kim to the couch in the living room, Betty started asking questions. "Do you hurt anywhere?"

"No, I'm just very tired, and my body hurts."

Immediately Betty started looking for answers. Placing her hand on the child's forehead, the mother could tell she did not have a fever. Neither did she have chills. And there was no stomach pain. The puzzled mom told Kim to lie on the couch for a while and see how she felt later. Without arguing, Kim laid on the couch, dozing often. By late afternoon she was feeling much better and was up playing with her little sister. Just a touch of the flu, Betty thought.

The next morning Kim went off to school feeling fine, but by early afternoon, she came back home looking slightly worse than the day before. She was zapped of all energy and went directly to the couch. Again, she dozed all afternoon, and by dinner she was feeling better.

This routine went on for a few days. Kim was coming home earlier and earlier, eventually appearing at the front door at lunchtime. Betty made an appointment with their family physician, Mr. Walter Bennett. If she couldn't figure it out, perhaps he could.

A thorough examination of Kim's general health caused Dr. Bennett to shake his head and stand in deep thought. "I don't know," he said. "Her symptoms are not the ordinary symptoms of the flu, but I don't know what else it could be. Let's assume for now that it is the flu. Here is a prescription for some antibiotics that should help. Make sure she takes them as directed, and watch her for a few more days."

The antibiotics seemed to help. After three days Kim's energy level seemed to pick up, and she did not come home early from school. By the time the antibiotics were finished, she was almost back to her old self. She rested more and was quieter than usual, but there was definitely a great improvement.

A week went by after the antibiotics were gone, and Betty's daily routine was back in place. Cleaning, cooking, washing, and ironing. Cleaning, cooking, washing and ironing. She was such a good wife and mother. One afternoon she was in the basement moving the clothes from the washer to the dryer when she heard the doorbell. She hurried up the stairs to the door. There stood Kim.

"What's the matter, Honey?" the concerned mother asked.

"I don't feel good, Mama," the worn-out girl replied. "I need to lie down."

Betty was very surprised, as her daughter had been doing so well after taking the antibiotics. As questions entered her mind, the mother began checking for a fever and chills. Neither was present. "Do you hurt anywhere?"

"No. I'm just tired, and my body aches," the eleven-year-old child said as she headed for the living room couch.

Betty was bewildered. These were the same complaints she had had last time. "You lie here, and I am going to call Dr. Bennett and see if maybe you need more antibiotics."

Betty picked up the phone and called the physician's office. The nurse got the family doctor on the phone immediately. After listening to Betty's account of Kim's health over the last couple of weeks, he asked her to bring Kim to his office. Betty called Larry, and they were on their way to the doctor's office in no time.

"I think perhaps she never actually was cured from the flu," the doctor explained. "Once the antibiotics wore off, it was still present and has returned in full force. Take this prescription to the pharmacy. It is a different type of antibiotic that is stronger and is taken over a longer period of time. To get her a jump start, right now I'll give her a shot of this same antibiotic."

Betty and Larry agreed and were happy to take their daughter home to rest. Sure enough, after resting and taking her medicine, she was up and back to her old self within a few days. She was even better than she had been after taking the previous antibiotic. She was energetic, playful, and getting involved with the activities at school. Betty was glad her daughter was up and well. The thoughts of something serious being wrong with Kim vanished from her mind.

Three weeks later the doorbell rang again. It was Kim, pale and lifeless. Over the course of the next few days, Kim gradually became sicker and sicker, so her parents returned to the doctor's office. Still Dr. Bennett could not come up with any answers. "Her blood test shows that her white blood cell count is slightly elevated. I think you should take her to the cardiologist and let him assess her."

The family's beloved Dr. Ziegler had moved to another city. This was difficult for the family to accept, as he had been their heart caregiver from the beginning. It was disheartening to have to turn their daughter's care over to someone new, but there was no choice. Dr. James Matthews was the one to examine her now.

While having his back to Betty and Larry, he asked, "How long ago was Kim's blood test?" The doctor was making notes on Kim's medical chart.

"Four weeks ago," Larry answered. "She finished her antibiotics three weeks ago."

The doctor removed his glasses from the top of his head, putting them in place for reading. His brows came together in the form of a frown. "According to the records you brought with you, her white blood cell count was high," he said, looking very thought provoked. "Let's do another blood test and compare them."

Kim sat up on the exam table trembling. "Does that mean another needle?" she asked tearfully.

Larry came over to stand by his daughter's side and hold her hands. "Yes, but it has to be done to find out why you're so sick." The eleven-year-old started crying little tears that flowed rapidly down her cheeks, but she did not say a word while the blood was drawn.

By the time the cardiologist returned to the room, Kim was lying calm, but tears still rolled from her eyes. Dr. Matthews looked to the floor, tapping the stem of his glasses against his teeth. Kim's curious parents waited for him to speak. "Kim's white blood cell count has escalated quite a bit in the last week. Has she had any dental work done lately?"

Larry and Betty looked one to the other. "Yes," Larry remembered. "She had a filling put in about seven weeks ago."

Dr. Matthews shook his head. "Did she premedicate for that procedure?"

"No," the father said, staring at the cardiologist. "Why?"

"Any dental work that causes the gums to bleed in any way can allow bacteria to get in the bloodstream, which can cause bacterial endocarditis. Bacterial endocarditis occurs when that bacteria enters the bloodstream and clings to the heart, inflaming the lining of the heart." The parents listened carefully as the doctor explained all about endocarditis and that Kim's white blood cell count indicated she had this infection. "Strong intravenous antibiotics are necessary. We will keep her here for six weeks to administer the antibiotics. She will have an IV the entire six weeks, as well as three shots each morning and evening."

Kim's face showed instant panic. She looked at her mother and father pleadingly. "What does that mean?"

Dr. Matthews looked at the little girl with empathy, while Larry started to explain that she would have to stay in the hospital for six weeks to get the medicine she needed. "They have to give you the medicine through a needle in your arm."

Terror ripped through the little girl's long body. I have to stay here by myself for six weeks, she thought. No way. A needle for six weeks? "Do you get to stay with me?" she asked of her mother.

"No, Honey, we don't. Adults are not allowed to stay. But don't worry. There will be nurses to take care of you when we aren't here. And I'm sure you will meet children to play with." Her mother tried to comfort her.

Dr. Matthews pursed his lips. "We have a nice game room, Kim. When you have been here a few days, you will start feeling better, and you can go there and play."

The nervous, sobbing eleven-year-old did not accept that as an important consolation. She continued to cry in fear.

Chapter Fifteen

Betty stood next to Kim in the examining room, squinting while the middle-aged nurse worked hard to get an intravenous line started in Kim's arm. The tiny veins would hide and roll, which made them difficult to find. The poor girl was crying uncontrollably. The nurse continued to poke and prod in several places. Kim looked around and found her mother's face. She cast sharp, pleading glares in her mother's direction. Betty's first instinct was to stop the nurse, pick up her child, and cuddle her. She even considered snatching her up and taking her home to protect her. In reality Betty knew her daughter was going to be all right and was getting the best care possible. It was just hard to watch.

The nurse excused herself for a minute and went to get help. Soon two additional nurses paraded into the room where the little girl was lying, her crying turning to strong sniffles. One of the nurses leaned over Kim and looked her in the eyes. "Honey, I know this hurts, but we have to get an IV started so that you can get your medicine," the head nurse explained. "Mom, sometimes children do better when their parents are not in the same room. Would you mind stepping out into the hall, please?"

Betty stepped sideways out into the hallway and closed the door behind her, positioning herself so she could see into the workroom window. It appeared that things were going better. Within just a few minutes, the exam-room door opened, and Kim walked out with the IV in place, a long pole (later named Irving) in tow. She was not exactly smiling, but the tears were all spent

Larry had been nervously watching for his wife and daughter from the family waiting room. As soon as he caught up with them, he leaned over and gave his daughter a consoling hug. "How are you doing, kiddo?" he asked, trying to assure himself more than her that everything was fine.

"It hurts," Kim frowned.

"You'll be all right," her dad told her. He gave her shoulder a slight squeeze of encouragement.

The tall, dark-skinned nurse guided the threesome to the room to which Kim had been assigned. She helped Kim put away what little she had brought with her and then offered a tour of the pediatric floor. "The visiting hours are 9:00 AM to

8:00 PM. You can call the nurses station anytime. Remind me to give you that phone number before you leave.

"This is the playroom," the nurse said, pointing off to the right. "It is next to the nurses station so that we can monitor the activity in there. Kim, there are many good games in that blue closet, and you can get them out anytime.

"Over here on the right is the snack room. Parents are allowed to help themselves to anything in there, including coffee. Our patients are not allowed in there unless accompanied by an adult."

Betty and Larry were becoming somewhat comfortable with leaving their daughter at the hospital. The nurses were nice, and there were activities to keep her busy. They thanked their tour guide and made their way down the hall to tuck Kim in bed. Visiting hours were almost over.

Feeling a little better, but still lying in her hospital bed, Kim was all smiles when her parents arrived the next day with her brother and sister. She had been too tired to get up today and was glad for the company.

"Hi," her little sister greeted her as she approached the hospital bed. She stood staring at the tall pole and the long tube that was connected to Kim's arm. The younger girl pointed at all the tape wrapped around her sister's wrist. "What's that?" she wanted to know.

Kim proudly held up her arm with the IV as if it were her best friend. "That's my IV," she explained. "That's how the nurses give me medicine through a needle in my arm."

Shaun continued to stare. "It's a shot they leave in your arm?" the young one with golden locks asked.

"Sort of," Kim nodded. "And this," she said as she pointed up above her head, "is Irving, my IV pole."

Shaun's head bobbed up and down in understanding. "Oh," was all she could say.

"Mom said you are going to be in here for Christmas," Brent said, approaching the bed and joining in the conversation.

The young patient's facial expression changed completely as the reality of his statement penetrated her mind. "Yeah," she acknowledged, "but Mom and Dad said we would make it special somehow."

"We're going to bring the presents here so we can open them together," Brent informed his sister.

Betty listened in on her children's conversation from across the room. Seeing the three of them together soothed her soul.

Within just a few days, Kimberly's health improved dramatically. She began getting acquainted with her roommate and other patients. It didn't take long before the children learned to gather in each other's rooms to play and watch television. The more the children got to know each other, the more work the nurses had on their hands. Wheelchair races clogged the halls, apple juice was turned into "specimens," the game room was louder than normal, and children were hard to find when it was time for medications. These children were sick, but that definitely did not deter their childish pranks.

The week before Christmas, some friends of the Vintons stopped by the hospital to bring Kim the small, decorated Christmas tree they had promised. The tree was two feet tall with small, twinkling lights and colorful miniature Christmas balls. It stood in the corner of the window, illuminating the room; a silver star trimmed the top. The hospital room immediately radiated a special mood, declaring that the Christmas festivities could now begin.

On Christmas Eve several groups from local churches and other organizations brought gifts for each pediatric patient. Then on Christmas morning, Santa Claus was the first visitor, with several gifts in his bag for one and all. Even though Kim didn't believe in Santa, it gave the day a special touch.

On Christmas afternoon, after attending the morning worship celebration of Jesus' birth, the Vinton family came to the hospital. They brought all of the Christmas gifts that were "to Kim" and "from Kim." The small, decorated tree and the gifts were moved to the lobby of that floor. Brent, Kim, and Shaun exchanged gifts between themselves and their parents. Of all the great times Kim had had with her new hospital friends and visitors, the Christmas day festivities etched themselves in her mind.

One day three weeks later, Dr. Matthews stepped into her hospital room. His grin from ear to ear told both the patient and her mother that good news was about to be announced. The heart doctor walked over to the bed to listen to Kim's chest and back, asking her to breathe deep several times as he listened to her lungs. The smile never left his face.

The doctor rose up from stooping over the eleven-year-old, walked over to Betty, and shook her hand. "You have a lucky girl here, Mrs. Vinton. When people are diagnosed with endocarditis, our first concern is what strain of bacteria is present in the bloodstream. According to the blood tests, Kim's strain was not one that could have damaged her heart. She has responded well to the antibiotics. We are going to release her to go home today."

Kim and her mom smiled at each other. This was the day they had been waiting for. Betty shivered slightly with excitement. Kim's feelings didn't show. Definitely she was thrilled with the idea of no more IVs and shots. At the same time, she had become so familiar with her surroundings and friends. As mother and daughter walked down the hall to leave, Kim looked back one last time. In a way she was really going to miss being here.

Chapter Sixteen

Getting back into the regular school schedule took a little time. Kim's thoughts were still back at the hospital with her friends. She missed them and the nurses who had been so nice, but as she worked hard to get caught up with her subjects at school, she slowly fell back into the routine of being a sixth grader, even receiving A's on her quarterly report card.

St. Matthew was a great school. It was small, and there were four grades per room. There were only five children in the sixth grade. "Class," her teacher Mrs. MacKenzie announced, "we are going across the hall for music in a few minutes. When we are done practicing the hymns and folk songs, fifth grade will come back here for study hall. Sixth grade will stay in the music room with the seventh and eighth grade and the high school students.

"This year we have decided to allow the sixth grade to be in the annual operetta performance. Today we are going to start learning the music for *The Pirates of Penzance.*"

Kim was thrilled! That was something she had always wanted to do. She was actually going to get to participate. She couldn't wait to find out about the part she would play.

That night after dinner, Larry and Betty began talking with the children about their news. Everyone had finished eating, and the table had been cleared. "Mom and I have something to tell you," Larry began. "As you already know, in January I will be graduating from the seminary. That means all of my schooling will be done and my ministry will begin. We have gotten a letter from a congregation in Marietta, Georgia. They want us to move down there so I can be their pastor."

The children looked from one to the other. They understood what that meant, but they were waiting for more details.

Larry continued, "In a few weeks, while you are on your Easter vacation, we will go down to Marietta to see where we will live. I will be conducting the Easter Sunday services. When school gets out for the summer, we will move."

This news brought on a mixed reaction from the children. Brent didn't really say much, but his mother suspected he was not anxious to move away from the school and friends to which he was attached. Moving in the summer after the ninth grade would not be an easy adjustment for him.

Kim didn't say much either. At the time she was glad that she would be able to participate in an operetta before they left. That was going to be so much fun!

Shaun was only five years old and in kindergarten. She was too young to really form an opinion. She would just "go with the flow."

Kim searched through the house, calling out for her mother. Spotting her in the kitchen, the young girl approached. "Mom," she said, "guess what?"

Betty turned around from peeling potatoes at the sink. "What, Honey?"

"Mom," Kim started over excitedly, "I got the part of the lead policeman in the operetta. I only have one line, but I also get to lead my class on and off the stage."

Betty rinsed her hands, smiled, and reached down to give her daughter a hug. "That's great!" I bet Mrs. MacKenzie gave her that part because she knew this was our last year, she thought to herself. How kind! "Do you know what Brent is going to be?" the mother asked.

"Yes," Kim answered. "He is going to be a pirate. He will be right up front on stage too." Betty grinned at her daughter's enthusiasm. It was fun to see her so happy after she had been so sick.

For months the school children practiced their parts and music. Betty and her friends worked hard making costumes. The stage scenery was painted. The choreography was written. Finally Mrs. MacKenzie brought it all together: the music, the costumes, the stage scenery, and the children's parts. The operetta was about to begin.

Larry, Betty, and Shaun sat in the audience as the lights went down and the play began. It was amazing how many lines the high school students had learned and how much music the grade school children could retain. Seeing the whole operetta play out was amazing. Before they knew it, the first half was over.

Larry went to the concession stand and got Shaun some popcorn during the break. Soon the lights were flashed several times. The second half was about to begin. The spectators took their seats as the opening music was played.

Just into the second half, Kim lead her line of policemen through the back door of the auditorium, down the middle isle, and up onto the stage. She was singing her heart out. She was so excited that tears even stung her eyes. Her mother and father were in the audience as proud as they could be. What a way to end four wonderful years at St. Matthew!

Four weeks later, on June 13, 1972, Larry graduated from the Martin Luther Institute of Sacred Studies Seminary. His family sat in the pews of the church, proud to be witnessing the result of God's calling and their dad's/father's hard work. He had spent many hours studying, writing sermons, and teaching at the parochial school. All of it was coming to an end. In just one hour, he would be Reverend Larry D. Vinton, and next week they would be moving to Marietta.

Chapter Seventeen

In August of 1972, shortly after Kim had reached the age of twelve, she and Betty found themselves in the office of Dr. William Plauth for a checkup with her new cardiologist.

"Can you start by giving me a summary of Kim's heart health to this point?" Dr. Plauth asked. He was a quiet, soft-spoken gentleman with a caring love that radiated from his eyes. He listened attentively, showing deep interest in Betty's review of Kim's birth, heart diagnosis, surgeries, and current condition.

"What types of activities do you enjoy, Kim?" the cardiologist asked the patient directly.

"I like to play the piano, ride my bike, and play in the water at the lake," she replied, nervously swinging her arms and legs.

"Can you run?" he asked.

This was not a question that the young, shy girl liked to answer. "Yes, but not very far. It makes me breathe hard, and that makes my lungs hurt. I have to stop and rest a lot."

"I see." The cardiologist rubbed his chin, shifted his glasses, and continued. "How old are you?"

"Twelve."

Dr. Plauth turned back toward Betty, who was fixing her skirt so that it hung properly from the chair that she was sitting in. She looked up just in time to see Dr. Plauth looking mysteriously at the floor, then at her. "Has she had any problems recently?"

"What kind of problems?"

"Does she turn blue more easily than she used to? Have you noticed her nails or lips turn blue more often? Does she show any unwarranted signs of fatigue?"

"No. Nothing comes to mind."

The cardiologist rose from the chair he had been leaning back in and pulled fresh paper over the examination table. "Kim, why don't you hop up here and let me take a listen."

The young girl followed the doctor's directions. She had already put on the hospital gown and was anxious to get the whole ordeal over with. The doctor lifted his stethoscope from his shoulders to her chest and placed the end pieces carefully into his ears. Embarrassed that the stethoscope needed to be placed all over her bare chest, Kim looked down at the floor. Placing the prewarmed, round end of the medical instrument on Kim, he concentrated on each sound. His eyebrows lifted as he listened.

"That's quite a swishing sound you have there," he observed. Then he placed the stethoscope on her back. Kim let out a sigh of relief that the first part of her examination was over. Having to expose herself was very embarrassing. The cardiologist was having her breathe in deeply to check her lungs. When he completed his evaluation, he patted Kim on the back and sent her to get dressed.

When all three of them were sitting back in their original seats, Dr. Plauth picked a piece of red lint from his jacket and began verbalizing his assessment. "All the sounds that I hear are what I would expect from a heart with a single left ventricle. The two Blalock shunts sound as though they are working well. In fact, they almost sound too good. By now we would have expected her to be having problems that would result in more surgery, but all seems well. Keep a close eye on her stamina and her fingernail, toenail, and lip color. Watch for blueness to appear more often. If you see any changes in her condition, please give me a call. Otherwise, she's doing great and does not need to come back for a year. Do you have any questions?"

"Not that I can think of," the smiling mom answered, picking up her purse and standing to leave.

Immediately upon arriving home, Kim ran off to play, and Betty sought out her husband to tell him the good news. "We just need to keep an eye on her and call the doctor if she has any changes," Betty said. "He is really nice and thorough. You're going to like him."

Both Larry and Betty monitored their daughter's health continually but allowed her to live a normal life. Her heart condition didn't change from one doctor visit to another. She was now in the seventh grade, and the only differences between her and the rest of the students were her hidden scars and the fact that she did not have to take physical education because she couldn't do the required exercises. Other than that, she was a normal child with minor limitations. Her parents were thankful for that.

One year blended into another. At the age of fifteen, Kim was becoming more and more independent. She had her first job and was participating in extra-curricular activities at school. As a sophomore in high school, she was president of her Junior Achievement Company, belonged to the foreign language club, sang in the advanced choir, attended many of the high school performances, and taught the youngest Sunday school class at church.

All this while, Kim's cardiologist was keeping detailed records of her activities and her overall well-being. When she reached the age of sixteen and was still without any signs of the projected ill health that warranted surgery, Dr. Plauth began to worry. He had kept track of her as closely as possible, but there had been no apparent change. He had to be missing something. She should have needed another surgery by now, he thought. Wanting to make sure that his diagnosis was right, the bewildered doctor took Kim's medical chart and headed to the adult congenital heart doctor across the street at Emory University, Dr. Robert Franch.

The two met in Dr. Franch's cluttered office. Medical files and reels of film were piled on his desk and bookcase, waiting to be reviewed. "How are you today?" Dr. Plauth inquired. "Thank you for taking the time to meet with me. The seemingly good health of this patient has me wondering if I am misdiagnosing her."

Dr. Franch smiled, but concern also showed on his face. Shaking Dr. Plauth's hand, he directed him to a comfortable chair. "What do we have here, Bill?" he asked.

"This sixteen-year-old female patient has a single ventricle with a double inlet and pulmonary artresia. She has had two Blalock-Taussig shunts done, one in 1960 at age three months and the other in January of 1965. The study of congenital heart disease is not advanced, and we are in the pioneer stages of treating children with this disease, but common sense and what little statistics we have show that she should be needing a third shunt of some kind by now."

The pediatric cardiologist opened Kim's medical chart for Dr. Franch's review. After giving him a few moments to study the chart thoroughly, Dr. Plauth began his line of questioning. "Am I missing something?" Dr. Plauth asked his colleague. "She's almost sixteen. Surely with the growth of her body, her heart needs some kind of surgical assistance." Dr. Franch continued to peruse all of the medical notes and documentation listed on Kim's chart.

"I can see why you would come to that conclusion. How old is she again?" Dr. Franch asked, flipping back to the front page. "Sixteen? And her last surgery was in 1965? Wow! How long has she been your patient?"

"Since 1972," Dr. Plauth informed the cardiologist. "In all it's been four years that I've had her as a patient. Her physical condition has not changed during that time."

"I don't see anything to tell us differently. But you're right. It seems impossible." Dr. Franch started back at the beginning of the medical chart, scouring it one last time for any possible information he may have missed the first two times. When he was done, he shrugged his shoulders in disbelief. "Maybe we should send her for a second opinion," he said.

"Do you have a place in mind?" Dr. Plauth asked.

"Yes. What do you think of sending her to Mayo Clinic? Right now it is the leading hospital for congenital heart defects. We don't want to take any chance that we are missing something."

Dr. Plauth nodded in confirmation. "I agree. Kim is coming in for an appointment next week. I'll talk to her parents then."

On the Thursday of her appointment, Dr. Plauth went through the regular routine of listening to Kim's heart and lungs, comparing what he heard to the notes he had made previously. He still agreed with Dr. Franch. The child needed to get a second opinion.

The cardiologist sat back in his chair. "Have you noted any change in Kim's health?"

"No," Betty responded. "My husband and I have both watched and compared notes. There appears to be no change."

"*Appears.* Good choice of words. Since appearances can be deceiving, I have been reviewing Kim's chart over and over looking for any changes over the last few years. Nothing is *appearing* to be wrong, while all common sense and statistics tell us she should need more surgery soon. I even took her chart over to Dr. Franch, the adult cardiologist across the street at Emory. He and I agree that Kim should get a second opinion from specialists who are especially trained in congenital heart defects."

"Do you have someplace in mind?" the contemplating mother wanted to know.

"Yes. We think Mayo Clinic in Rochester, Minnesota, would be the best place to go. It has state-of-the-art medical machinery. The staff there may be able to detect something that we haven't."

Betty considered the cardiologist's words. She and Larry had never met anyone with a heart defect except Kim. It had been a somewhat lonely parenting road—handling their child's delicate condition with no one to compare notes. They relied totally on the doctors' instructions.

Dr. Plauth stood and leaned against the examination table that sat along the wall. "Mayo Clinic is a great place. It has a good cardiac care unit. The cardiologists may not find anything different than what we have, but it is better to be safe than sorry.

The mother took all of the information in, looked at her daughter, and then looked back at the cardiologist. "I'll talk to my husband when I get home. When do you think we should go?"

"It's not an emergency, but the sooner the better."

When Betty and Kim got home and Larry was finished with his counseling session, both parents sat on the couch and shared the events of their day. Larry went first, then Betty. "So they want us to take her to Mayo Clinic for a second opinion," she concluded.

"What do you think about that?" Larry asked, as he brushed her cheek with the back of his hand.

"Logically the doctor's concerns are valid. At the same time, we have to carefully weigh the expense and the amount of time you can be gone from the congregation."

Larry already had those details worked out in his head. "If this can be turned into a family camping experience and we're gone less than two weeks, I know the people of the church will understand."

A few weeks later they packed their family in the car with the pop-up camper behind it and headed for Minnesota.

Chapter Eighteen

Riding in the car that far was not fun, but stopping to visit friends along the way helped bring enjoyment to their travel. Betty worked hard to keep the children entertained by talking to them and playing children's car games with them. "I see a cow," Shaun shouted. "That's ten points." Shaun let everyone know that she was gaining the lead in the "I spy" game they were playing.

"Well, I saw a graveyard on your side too," Kim interjected, "and that is worth minus twenty-five."

"Is not," Shaun shouted back.

"Is too, isn't it, Mom?" the older sister insisted.

"Kim, leave Shaun alone. No one else saw the graveyard, so it doesn't count." The mother of the two fighters put the differences to an end. "Did you know that both of your sets of grandparents are going to meet us in Rochester?" The wise woman in the front seat tried to distract them.

"Why are they coming?" Kim wanted to know.

"In case you have surgery. They want to be there with all of us."

"Oh," the teenager replied quietly. Knowing that she was scheduled for a catheterization and possibly surgery was serious enough; but the news about her grandparents coming intensified her fears and anxiety. Nervousness played with her heart and soul.

Two days later Larry, Betty, and Kim got up early and drove to Mayo Clinic, while Brent and Shaun stayed with their grandparents, who had already arrived. An employee at the information desk saw that the threesome looked perplexed and helped them find their way around. By the time they went to lunch, the urine test, blood work, X ray, electrocardiogram, and echocardiogram were completed.

After lunch the three joined the cardiologist in his office. He already had the results of the tests. "The tests we have done so far do not indicate any anatomical changes in Kim's heart and its function," the doctor began. "This is good news. But like your cardiologists in Atlanta, we are perplexed that Kim hasn't needed further surgery. We want to make sure that her heart is functioning okay by doing a heart catheterization."

Kim started sniffling. The only thing she could think about was the pain. Her thoughts were a little beyond reality. The only pain she would feel was when they inserted the catheter. After that there was none. Nonetheless, she could not stop her tears.

Both her parents and the cardiologist felt bad about what the girl was going through. "I'll tell you what, Kim," the doctor told her, "even though it is not a common practice, you can sleep through the whole thing."

The scared patient nodded in agreement.

Shortly after the catheterization was completed, the cardiologist talked to the nervous parents.

"Incredible!" he reported. "She is at the best function of anyone I've seen with such a complex heart defect. We don't know why or how, but everything looks great. There is no need to do anything at this point. Continue to have her checked frequently by her cardiologist, and if anything comes up, we'll be here to help."

Betty and Larry glanced at one another. They knew how Kim was doing so well. The Lord Jesus had promised to be with them always. Both parents and especially Kim were relieved to know that there was no treatment or surgery in the foreseeable future. As soon as Kim was released, they drove to the hotel where the rest of the family was gathered. Everyone was anxious to hear the news.

"Kim is doing amazingly well, and nothing needs to be done at this time," Betty announced. Cheers and applause invaded the room.

Kim had words of her own. "I'm tickled pink!" she exclaimed in joy. The pun made everyone in the room laugh. That statement made her mother realize how truly scared her daughter had been.

Larry got everyone's attention and spoke. "Let's bow our heads and thank the Lord for this wonderful news!"

Chapter Nineteen

After the visit to Mayo Clinic, Kim continued to take her cardiologists' advice and moved another step toward claiming her independence in her health care decisions. As difficult as it was on her parents, they wanted her to start this process of growing up while she was still living at home. They would have an opportunity to watch her take over her own health care and yet be with her on a day-to-day basis to educate and encourage her in the right direction. The doctor could be easily contacted if they had any concerns.

One afternoon Kim approached her mother with a request. "I think it's time for me to start taking the independent route Dr. Plauth and Dr. Franch talk about so much. Would it be okay if I started going to the doctor by myself?"

Betty's mind reeled with reasons why Kim shouldn't go alone. Her stomach churned with knots. Then Dr. Plauth's words echoed in her ear: "All children look forward to growing up and becoming independent adults. Don't hold Kim back and turn her into an invalid."

Betty took a deep breath. "Why do you need to go to the doctor?"

"I'm just going to the dentist. They are going to evaluate the work that needs to be done on my teeth, but they won't work on them until next time, when I will premedicate."

"Okay. Just make sure they don't stick any sharp objects in your mouth until you have premedicated."

Kim rolled her eyes. "I know, Mom. I won't. See ya later."

Tears formed in Betty's eyes as the reality of what was happening rushed over her. She had been totally in charge of Kim's care since she was born. Now it was time to let her go and grow. Letting her daughter cut the proverbial "apron strings" was not going to be easy, but what a joy to watch her become an independent, self-sufficient adult, especially when the doctors had originally predicted that her infant would not live to be a month old. God has blessed them!

Kim sat in the lobby looking at a magazine while waiting to be taken back to see the dentist. The dental hygienist called the teenager's name and led her to one of the work spaces. She informed Kim that she was going to start by cleaning her teeth. Kim sat up and shook her head. "No. I have to premedicate first."

The hygienist gave the seventeen-year-old girl a funny look. "No, you don't," she assured the young patient.

"Yes, I do." Kim was more adamant this time.

"No, you don't," the hygienist argued, shaking her head and reviewing the doctor's instructions.

Kim sat up further and explained about her heart condition and bacterial endocarditis. The hygienist gave a loud huff and argued some more. "I'll go ask the doctor."

Within a few minutes the hygienist came back, leaned Kim's chair back, and started working. "The doctor said that having a cleaning will be fine." The concerned teenager could feel the tears dripping into her ears as the hygienist leaned her way back and began her work. All of the other doctors made such a clear insistence about taking medication before dental work, but apparently this dentist did things differently. Hopefully he was right!

Arriving home with a clean and refreshed smile, Kim sought out her mother to let her know the details of her visit to the dentist. Her mother showed a slight frown and look of concern, but she didn't say a word.

Kim lay on the bathroom floor. "Mom," she called, "help me!" Her mother came running from the kitchen where she had been working on the lunch dishes.

"What's the matter, Dear? Why are you lying on the floor?"

"Mom, something's wrong! I can hardly lift my head up. My body aches, I'm chilled, my energy is zapped, and now I'm throwing…" Kim stopped in midsentence to empty her stomach. When the wave of nausea passed, she continued. "I can't stop throwing up."

Betty wrung her hands in worry. She had noticed that Kim's stamina had dropped and her energy level had reached an all-time low. The mother's heart showed compassion and concern at the same time. Her daughter's health was slowly deteriorating. What if it was her heart? What if she went to the doctor and found out it was time for her third surgery? These thoughts had flowed through her mind several times a day. Now Kim was throwing up. Something had to be done.

"Larry, we need to do something," Betty called out to her husband. "Kim is so sick she can hardly get up off the floor to throw up. We've got to get her some help!"

Larry stuck his head into the bathroom to size up the situation. "What should we do?"

"Let's go to the emergency room," the mother suggested.

"But which emergency room?" Larry fervently tried to figure out the best plan. "Do we take her to the local emergency room, where they won't know much, if anything, about congenital heart defects? Or do we make the trip down to Egleston in Atlanta? Do her symptoms seem flu-like, or could it be her heart? This is always the dilemma we have."

Betty knew her husband was right. Every time Kim wasn't feeling well, it was easy to assume it was her heart. This time was no different. They had to make a decision to the best of their ability and go from there. "Larry, if we're not sure and she is this sick, let's take her to the closest emergency room. They can always transfer her to Egleston if they think it is necessary. At least they will be able to give her something for her stomach."

"You're right," the father agreed. "Egleston is too far to go. Whatever we decide, we need to do it right now. She's going to become dehydrated soon."

Betty touched her husband on the arm. Knowing he was there gave her strength. "Can you find Brent and Shaun? I need to give them instructions to follow while we are gone."

A short time later, Brent and Shaun stood in the kitchen asking their mother what was going on. "Your sister is sick. We need to take her to the hospital. Brent, we probably won't be home in time, so here is your dinner. Just warm it up in that saucepan when you're ready. We'll call you and tell you how things are going."

Brent nodded in assent. Shaun, on the other hand, thought she was forgotten about. "What about me?"

"Dad and I have changed our minds. You are going with us. Go get your shoes on and get in the car. We'll be right there."

Larry walked into the bathroom, scooped his daughter's body off the floor, and placed her carefully in the car. In moments the foursome was on their way to the hospital.

The local hospital waiting room was filled with people. Larry looked for a place for Kimberly to lie down during the wait. When the receptionist realized his predicament, she motioned for him to bring Kim to a room in the back where there would be more privacy.

A doctor appeared quickly. He had a special place in his heart for children, and this was no exception. "How long has she been like this?" he asked, while giving Kim's body a once-over. "Her fingernails are blue. Let me listen to your heart, Kim."

Before Betty or Larry had a chance to explain about Kim's heart condition, the doctor was listening to her heart pump. He brought his brows together and looked to the ceiling, as if it might give him the answer to what was going on. "The sound of her heart is unusual, isn't it?" he stated.

"She has a heart defect. She has only one ventricle, and that ventricle has a double inlet." Both parents responded, one after the other.

"How long has she been sick?" the physician asked, still looking at the ceiling in deep thought.

Betty responded hesitantly. "Well, she has slowly been more and more tired over the last week or so. She doesn't have a fever, but neither does she have any energy. She just started being sick to her stomach late this morning."

"Can you think of any connection between her symptoms and her heart?" the doctor asked.

"No. In fact, we struggled over the decision of coming here or taking her to Egleston. We never know what is going to be the right thing to do." As if a fast-pitched ball was headed toward her, Betty's hand flew up to her mouth. "Kim had a dentist appointment a few weeks back and the doctor told her she didn't need to be premedicated for teeth cleaning." The mother could not escape the feeling of guilt that she hadn't thought of that sooner.

The doctor wasn't sure how that all fit together. A quizzical look spread across his facial features, his brow came down, and the ends of his mouth pulled back. Then a look of understanding came over his whole being. "Are we talking about the possibility of infection here?"

"Yes," Larry began. "Have you ever heard of bacterial endocarditis?"

"I think I have. Maybe I should go look it up."

"Heart patients can easily get bacteria in their bloodstreams during dental work. The bacteria flow through the bloodstream and then attach to the heart. It takes two to six weeks for the patient to begin having symptoms."

"Yes, I do know a little bit about that. How about if I order some lab work on her blood and see what we find? It will take a little bit of time, but we shouldn't do anything else until we know about that."

Thirty minutes passed by the time the nurse arrived to draw blood. Betty was trying to keep Shaun occupied, while Larry was tending to their other daughter. Kim's vomiting had now turned into dry heaves, the kind that come from deep within.

"What took so long?" Larry confronted the phlebotomist.

"I'm sorry, sir," she responded rather curtly. "We have been very busy."

Larry stopped, realizing he was taking the frustration of their situation out on the nurse. At the same time, it dawned on the nurse that it wasn't the father's fault that she had had a bad day. "I'm sorry, sir," the woman wearing the scrubs apologized. "I'll take this right down to the lab myself and hurry them along."

The father acknowledged his wrong words by nodding his head.

As soon as the nurse pulled the syringe out of the tool bin, Kim started to cry. Flashbacks from her last hospital stay came streaming into her head: the needles, the doctors, the poking, the prodding, and especially the IVs. She was tired of the problems her heart condition caused all the time. Her poor parents always had to take care of her illnesses. These depressing thoughts made her cry even harder.

The nurse cleared her throat to get Kim's attention. "Okay, Dear," the nurse spoke softly. "Just a little pinch and we'll be done." Kim knew better than "just a little pinch." Her thoughts and fears made it even worse, and Kim let out a yelp.

Larry came to his daughter's side immediately. "Here," he offered. "Hold my hand and squeeze when it hurts. You know you have to do this in order to get better."

Kim knew he was right, but tears still made their way out of her ducts and down her face, gathering on her chin until the nurse finished the task.

About an hour and fifteen minutes later, the doctor appeared carrying sheets of paper with letters and numbers marked on them. "The tests are back. Kim's white blood cell count is extremely high. This could be a sign of infection."

Both parents agreed without hesitation. "What can you do for her?"

"I think you should take her to Egleston Children's Hospital to see her cardiologist," the emergency physician told the apprehensive couple.

"Okay." Betty understood the doctor's hesitation to diagnose and treat her daughter. "As soon as she gets something for her vomiting, we'll be on our way."

The graying man smoothed the locks of hair hanging to the side of his forehead. "I can't give her anything. She should wait until the doctors at Egleston diagnose her so that her blood test is pure and clear of any medications. This is a copy of the blood work we did here in case it's needed"

Larry and Betty bundled up Shaun and Kim. The older sister was too weak even to put on her own coat, so the caring father lifted her up in his arms and set her in a wheelchair to make it to the car. Kim searched her father's eyes for answers. "Can't they help me?" she asked softly, tears coming to her eyes again.

"Yes, Honey," he assured her. "They have helped. There is an infection in your body somewhere, and he wants Dr. Plauth to treat you, since he is your cardiologist. They suspect it might be bacterial endocarditis."

Kim was admitted to Egleston Children's Hospital only a couple hours later. Dr. Plauth ordered a blood culture, which would show the type of bacteria that was present. It would take a few days for the culture to reveal the type of bacteria. The young patient would stay at Egleston until the results came back.

Chapter Twenty

The next morning Dr. Plauth walked into Kim's hospital room, surprised to see Betty there already. "Good morning, Betty. You're here rather early this morning!" The doctor greeted the caring mother in his gentle, quiet voice.

Betty smiled. "I'm going into work late. Is there any news?"

The cardiologist stepped forward to shake her hand and leaned against the bed while concentrating on Kim's medical chart. "I'm glad I caught you. Kim's blood report is already back. She has tested positive for bacterial endocarditis. Generally a culture takes one to several days to be read. Her blood culture started growing overnight."

Betty was sad but not surprised. She remembered her daughter's account of her trip to the dentist. A light sigh passed through her lips. "A six-week hospital stay, right?"

"Actually, recent studies have been done about these infections and the use of certain antibiotics. The medicines we now use can cut the stay down to four weeks."

This information brought a hint of relief to the concerned mother. Kim felt no such relief. Six weeks or four weeks, what was the difference? Those weeks were still full of IVs, shots, and bad food. The seventeen-year-old could not keep control of her emotions. She cried hard, dreading the coming month in the hospital. On top of being sick, she would miss part of her senior year of high school.

The doctor continued. "Dr. Franch and I have conferred about Kim's care. Both of us agree that because of Kim's age, she should be moved to Emory University, across the street, and be treated as an adult. Now seems like the perfect time for making an easy transition from pediatric to adult cardiology." Dr. Plauth paused for a moment so Betty could collect her thoughts. "She could be moved this morning."

Betty nodded in understanding. Making the transition now was logical. "Kim, how do you feel about that?" Betty asked. Kim was too sick to even have an opinion. Betty could tell it didn't matter to her daughter. "I'm leaving shortly," Betty said as she looked at Dr. Plauth. "Do you need me to do anything before I go?"

Dr. Plauth handed Betty some papers. "Please fill out these forms to approve moving Kim from Egleston to Emory. We will get the process started right away."

After completing all of the paperwork, Betty approached her daughter. "Kim, I have to go to work, but I'll come back this evening. Do you need anything?"

"Yes. Could you please call both of my employers and let them know that I won't be coming to work for awhile?" The sick patient scribbled down two phone numbers. "This one is for the construction company, where I work on weekdays." Kim pointed out the correct phone number. "Please tell Dennis that I won't be coming for a few weeks. I'll call him in a couple days. Also, could you please call Anita at Macy's and let her know the same? Hopefully she will be able to hold my positions for me."

A couple hours later, Kim was lying in a bed on the adult cardiology floor at Emory, thankful there was a tunnel connecting it to Egleston. The weather was sunny, but the temperature was cold. Being wheeled underground was great.

The nurses were still in her room getting her settled. They were all very nice and tried to help Kim feel comfortable even though her roommate and all the other patients were quite a bit older. Kim was thankful for the hospital workers' efforts to make this transition a pleasant one, but that did not take away the anxiety of knowing that IV needles would soon be inserted. On the outside she tried to be brave. On the inside she was terrified. Needles, needles, needles! Ugh! Memories from her last bout with endocarditis came flooding to her mind as tears trickled down her cheeks, and her anxiety intensified.

Eventually nurse Lynn came through the doorway, followed by…yes…Irving, the IV pole. Kim tensed up. Lynn smiled. "It's not that bad," she tried to encourage her young patient. "If you relax, it will be much easier. Otherwise your veins will shrink and roll, making them difficult to find."

While she talked, Lynn continued to get the medicine hooked up on the IV pole. "Now look the other way. You will feel a little prick, and we will be done." Because of her anxiety and uncooperative attitude, however, it took forty-five minutes, several needle sticks, and four nurses to finally get the IV started. As the ordeal went on, Nurse Lynn's heart went out to the young patient. This was a difficult time for the teenager.

When the whole IV-insertion experience was over, Kim commented on what a beautiful sapphire ring Lynn was wearing. The nurse smiled. "A boyfriend gave it to me," she explained. Then Lynn took off her very special sapphire ring and placed it on Kim's right ring finger. "If you like it that much, you should have it," she said to Kim. Kim felt somewhat stunned that someone she barely knew would do something so nice. As her stay lengthened and she got to know the nurses, she realized how special they really were.

One afternoon while lying in her hospital bed and watching *Gilligan's Island* for the gazzillionth time, Kim received a phone call. "Hi, Kim. This is Mr. Scott from the Junior Achievement main office. How are you?"

"I'm fine, thanks. These afternoon shows on television are getting boring though. The same shows are on day after day." Kim heard Mr. Scott chuckle. "How are you?" she asked.

"I'm doing well, thank you. I wanted to call and let you know that you will be able to keep your presidency in your Junior Achievement Company, even though you haven't been able to attend meetings lately. Your advisors agreed to let you remain president. That qualifies you for attending the President's Roundtable Convention at a college in Indiana. Are you interested in attending?"

Kim sat up straight in bed. "Really?"

"Yes. The conference is for the presidents of all the Junior Achievement Companies in the United States. This week-long seminar teaches participants how to become stronger leaders in the real world. Registration is due soon, so we are going to let your mother take care of that for you if you want to go."

"Sure, I do. That sounds great!"

"Okay," Mr. Scott said with a smile in his voice. "I thought you would, but I needed to check before I confirm you participation. Hurry up and get well. Your J.A. team is awaiting your return."

"I will, and thank you. Goodbye. And thanks again." Kim wanted to make sure she expressed her true appreciation.

"Goodbye." With that Mr. Scott hung up the phone.

Kim immediately got out of bed and dragged Irving with her to the nurse's station to share her news. The nurses were excited for her and congratulated her with hugs.

The rest of Kim's stay was a breeze. Even though the IVs had to be changed every three to five days, she learned to tolerate the pain and enjoyed the special attention from the nurses.

Chapter Twenty-One

Kim's return to school after the long absence did not go as smoothly as it had when she was younger. Most of her teachers understood her long absence, but her history teacher, Mrs. Cantrell, had no tolerance for papers being turned in late. As a senior, Kim's classes were more difficult, and it was hard for her to keep up with her schoolwork. The history teacher was adamant that she catch up within a week. That included writing a paper about a historical event. As hard as Kim tried, she found the task impossible.

The struggling student went to Mrs. Cantrell to discuss the problem and remind her that she was trying to catch up in other classes also. Mrs. Cantrell had no compassion. She simply gave Kim a slip to take home for her parents to sign and threatened to see that Kim did not graduate. The seventeen-year-old was normally submissive and obedient, but in this case she did not comply and did not take the note home. Instead, she turned her paper in the next week. Mrs. Cantrell reminded her how late the paper was and that the tardiness would be reflected in her grade for the course. And it was, but her parents didn't say anything when her report card arrived. Kim was relieved.

Kim had a great time at the President's Roundtable and throughout the rest of her senior year. It was full of new and exciting experiences, including dating, going out after the football games, dressing formally for the homecoming dances, attending the prom, and serving as an officer for different organizations. And now she was at the end of the year, getting ready to graduate.

The thought of graduating was sad in one way and happy in others. She would miss being involved in all of the activities. At the same time, she was now seventeen years old and excited about reaching yet another milestone. Since she had received a four-year, all-expenses-paid scholarship through Junior Achievement, the next phase of her life would be spent going to Kennesaw State College, which was only twenty minutes from home.

"Kimberly Jean Russell," the principle announced. Kim turned and looked up at her parents and grandparents before stepping up onto the stage to receive her diploma. Inside she was beaming with pride to have been a part of Sprayberry High School in Marietta, Georgia.

Kim's college days only lasted a year and a half. She hated giving up a full-ride scholarship that others could have used, but college was just not for her. She wanted to be in the workforce instead.

"I love working in retail," she told her friend. "But I want to have a job doing accounting. I love numbers."

Sarah nodded her head in understanding

"I filled out paperwork at an employment agency. The agent there called today, and I have an interview with Pepsi-Cola on Friday. The position is night auditor. I would be settling the route drivers' paperwork when they come back from delivering Pepsi to the retail shops."

"That sounds interesting. Let me know what happens."

"Sure will," Kim affirmed.

Kim walked into the small auditing office behind the gentleman who was interviewing her. "This is where you would work, and this is Carol. The two of you would be working together from 3 PM to 11 PM auditing drivers' paperwork." The gentleman then turned to Carol. "Carol, will you please give Kim one of the sheets to audit. I want to test her adding machine skills."

"Sure," Carol replied, while digging to the bottom of the stack she was working on. After pulling out the form she was trying to reach, she handed it to Kim, giving her a quick explanation about what needed to be done.

Kim's hands flew over the adding machine keys. Robert was very impressed. "Wow! You're quick. And your answer is correct too. That is great. You are exactly the person we need here."

Two days later Kim was hired as a night auditor at Pepsi-Cola. She worked in night audit for a few years and was eventually transferred to the main office in the accounts receivable department.

During this time Kim began dating a young man named Mike. Before long she realized he was not right for her. He was six feet tall with very fine features, but his personality did not match hers. She liked meeting people and getting out; he liked to stay home and do nothing. She went to church; he didn't. She was close to her family; he hardly ever saw his family unless his parents invited him over for dinner. There was no reason to try and make it work. "Sarah, I just don't know how to tell him," she confided to her best friend on their way home from the mall. "You know Mike gets angry easily."

"All the more reason to break up," Sarah pointed out. "Just meet him somewhere in public and tell him." Sarah was trying to motivate her friend to do what needed to be done. "Just face it! He's not right for you."

Kim pulled a mirror from her purse, fixed her hair, and checked her makeup. This whole issue upset her. What made breaking off a relationship so much work? Closing her compact and putting it back in its place, the rattled teenager tried to change the subject. Her shopping buddy beat her to it.

"Adam and I are going over to a friend's house tonight. Do you want to come?"

"And be the third wheel? No, thanks."

"Come on," Sarah pleaded. "We're just going over to see Tom and some other people for a little while. Go with us."

Kim hesitated and huffed audibly. She didn't want to do anything but go home, bury her head in her pillow, and cry, but she knew that was ridiculous. "All right. Pick me up on your way there."

Three hours later the threesome arrived at the party. "Kim, that's Tom sitting over there. He's Adam's best friend." Sarah was intent upon helping her good friend meet new people and have a good time. Kim looked toward Tom to size him up. He was tall with long brown hair. He had a mustache and a beard. Nothing about him was especially striking, but he seemed like a nice guy.

"We already know each other," Kim informed Sarah. "Tom and my brother are friends."

"Oh, okay. Then I'll be right back." Sarah wanted to talk to some other friends before the evening was over. Kim stood there alone, not knowing what to do.

Tom noticed Kim standing by herself, almost as if she was trying to avoid communicating with others. They were distant acquaintances, which made the circumstance even more awkward.

"You want to go downstairs with everyone else?" Tom asked, trying to be polite.

"No, thanks," Kim answered.

"What's the matter?" Tom wouldn't leave her alone.

"Nothing." she stated flippantly.

"Okay." Tom gave up. Obviously Kim was not interested in carrying on a conversation.

When he went back to reading, Kim coughed to get his attention. She didn't really know him, but neither did she want to be ignored.

"Are you okay?" the young man asked, staring at her.

"Yes."

"You look as though you're mad at the world. Do you want to talk about it?" Tom thought his efforts were pointless, but at least he was trying.

"I'm dating a guy that I want to break up with, but I don't know how," Kim answered, expecting the conversation to end there. But it didn't. Tom listened carefully, asked questions, and gave advice for the next forty-five minutes. All of his answers made sense. She knew now that she should just go and get it over with, but not until tomorrow afternoon. She needed one more day to get up her nerve. The next day was Saturday, and it would be convenient to meet up with him.

The meeting with Mike the next afternoon turned into a one-sided shouting match. "I can't believe you are doing this to me! You're just like the last girl I dated." He went on and on as his voice rose in decibels.

"I can't help what happened to you before. I just don't want to date anyone right now." By the time the words were out of her mouth, the door to the fast-food restaurant slammed shut and Mike was screeching out of the parking lot. That was not exactly the scenario she had hoped for, but at least the deed was done.

Over the next several weeks Kim and Sarah spent quite a bit of time with Adam and Tom, which often lead to Kim and Tom spending time alone. This made Kim nervous. She needed to be sure Tom knew that their friendship would never become anything more. "So I just want you to know right up front that even though we've spent a lot of time together because of Sarah and Adam, I am really not interested in being more than just friends. You're a great guy and a great listener, but I'm not interested in dating right now. As you know, I just got over a bad relationship, and I am not prepared to go through all of that again."

Tom listened while Kim explained her position on their relationship. "Good," he replied. "I'm not either. I hate the whole 'dating thing.'"

Kim felt as though she had been slapped in the face. What did he say? He's not interested either? How dare he! Of course he is interested. No guy was going to tell her he didn't like her! No, sir! All of a sudden Kim was aware of her thoughts. What was she thinking? Didn't she just get done telling him she was not interested? Yes, she did! Then why did it matter? Deep down, she knew she did not like being turned down. Who did he think he was? He was *not* going to do this to her.

Kim turned and looked Tom in the eyes, feeling as though there was smoke coming from her ears. "You don't like me? What's wrong with me?" One question after the other bounced out of her mouth without her even thinking about what was happening. Question by question their conversation covered all the reasons why they didn't want a relationship. The more Tom talked, the more interested Kim became. He did have a big heart! He was loving and kind and a great listener. She could talk to him about anything. In the back of her mind, she wondered what was happening. After all, she was not interested in a relationship…right? In spite of all the thoughts that were going through Kim's head, the two young people talked for a long time, their conversation easily flowing from topic to topic.

When they finally parted ways, they made arrangements to get together the next day. And when they parted that day, they made arrangements to get together the following day…and the following…and the following.

Chapter Twenty-Two

At the end of two weeks, Tom and Kim were inseparable. They visited friends, picked each other up after work, and spent time at Tom's house, talking for hours. One Friday night they were on their way home from visiting a friend who was camping. The route they took passed the same place where they had met two weeks before, the place where they had told each other they were not interested in dating. This time they knew each other better. Kim knew all about Tom, and Tom knew all about Kim, including her heart defect, all she had been through, and her uncertain future. They looked at each other. "You know, you're a very kind, loving person," Kimberly said. "I've really enjoyed our time together these last two weeks."

"Me too!" Tom replied, nervously fidgeting with his coat zipper. "Wasn't it just two weeks ago that we were here discussing the fact that we didn't want to date? Our time together has been short, but it has been so much fun. For some reason I think we are going to end up spending the rest of our lives together."

By now Kim was pulling her car away from the parking lot to head home. "I know what you mean. I think you're right. It's a weird feeling for only being together for a couple weeks. As far as spending the rest of our lives together, I don't know. Because of my heart problems, I have an uncertain future. We have no idea what's going to happen with my heart. My health is great right now, but the doctors keep saying I will have to have more surgery eventually. How long will my good health last? Some day I could begin having more problems. I would never want to burden someone with that. Plus, I can't bear children, remember?"

"I know your medical situation. There is no way to predict the future for anyone. God has taken care of you so far. Why not enjoy what we have and wait and see together? And as far as children, adoption is a great idea. Like you said when you were little, 'God has a special little girl picked out for me.' You don't need to worry about any of that. I know all about the baggage. And yes, I love you!" Tom reached over and gave her a small hug and kissed her on the cheek. Then he waited for her response, but she was deep in thought. He grabbed her right hand. "So what do you say?"

Kim looked up into Tom's adorable eyes. "I love you too. It's just unbeliev-able that we can feel this way after only two weeks."

"Does this make us engaged?" Tom was eager to stake his claim.

"If you're sure, but I think you should take some time to think it all through first."

"I have thought it all through. I love you, and we will go through every step together! Now, one more time, are we getting married?" Tom was persistent.

A tear slowly dripped down Kim's cheek. God is so good to me, she thought "If you are absolutely positive, yes! But we should probably wait a while to tell anyone. Let's give ourselves a couple months to get used to the idea first. Most people won't understand how it could happen so fast."

"That's probably a good idea," Tom agreed, even though he felt they were both very positive that they would someday marry. A kiss and hug ended the conversa-tion. After three months of dating, Tom decided to ask for Kim's hand in marriage. He went to the Vinton's home while Kim was at work. Tom joined Larry, who was sitting in the living room. As soon as Tom got up the courage to start speaking, Larry got up and went to the kitchen. Tom followed. Again the words were sitting on Tom's lips waiting to be released, when Larry made his way to the basement. This went on for several minutes, when Betty realized what was happening. "Larry," she said, "can you please sit down. Tom wants to talk to you."

All of a sudden Larry understood what was about to happen. Tom followed him back down to his office in the basement. After several minutes of conversa-tion about the commitment of marriage and Kim's heart condition, Larry gave them his blessing and April 24, 1981 was chosen for their wedding day.

On April 24, 1981, all of Tom's groomsmen were standing at the front of the church in their dark blue tuxedoes as the music began to play. The bridesmaids, wearing long flowing light blue dresses with lacy armed coverings and hats began their entry. The cute, precious flower girl and the ring bearer were next. Finally the wedding march began, and everyone stood. Kim's father dressed in his pasto-ral attire, took her by the arm to walk her down the aisle.

There had been much discussion about how this first part of the church ser-vice would go. It was special to be married by your father, but how was that sup-posed to play out? He couldn't leave her at the front and go up into the chancel to ask "Who gives this woman to be married to this man?" and then run back to answer. But weeks before the wedding, he had made a decision about how to handle it. He would not share it with anyone until the day of the wedding.

Here they were now, about to walk down the aisle. While the congregation was standing and before Kim and her dad took their first step, he leaned over to kiss her and say quietly, "I love you."

"I love you too, Dad!"

Then they started walking toward Tom, who stood at the front of the church. They stopped briefly so that Kim could give her mother a kiss. As they got to the front, the proud father looked his soon-to-be son-in-law in the eyes and began to speak. "Tom, it is with joy that Kim's mother and I give her hand to you in marriage. You are a very special addition to our family. May God bless your marriage, and may you live according to his will. May he guide both of you and keep you always in his care."

What a blessing to have her very own dad feel that way about the husband she was never sure she would have!

Chapter Twenty-Three

Ten months after they had returned from their honeymoon, Tom and Kim were sleeping late because they had both worked the night shift. At 9:10 AM their phone rang. Kim picked up the receiver.

"Hello?" she answered sleepily.

"Mrs. Russell?"

"Yes?" Kim replied with a curious tone in her voice.

"You don't know me, but someone you know told me that you are interested in adopting a child." This brought Kim right out of bed and onto her feet, while her husband woke up somewhat dazed.

"Are you still interested?"

By now Kim was shaking. A baby? Just dropped in our laps from heaven? While these thoughts were rushing around in her head, she put her hand over the receiver. "Tom, this lady wants to know if we are interested in adopting a baby."

This announcement made Tom bolt up straight in bed. "What? Who is she?"

"She is the friend of a friend of ours. She wants to know if we are interested in adopting a baby."

"Of course, we are!" Tom nearly shouted.

"Of course, we are!" Kim repeated.

The lady on the phone gave her some details and guidelines about the adoption.

Since the baby was not due for a few months, Kim and Tom had time to get well prepared. They shopped for baby items at garage sales, borrowed furniture and decorated the nursery. The soon-to-be parents were busy finishing the details in the nursery when the phone call came. Their daughter had been born. They could pick her up in a couple days.

Two days later the young, excited parents arrived at the hospital to pick up their little girl. Kim commented on how surprisingly calm she felt. That all changed the minute the hospital doors opened and she saw her new baby girl. She broke out in tears as the nurse handed her tiny daughter over to her. The proud father grinned from ear to ear, breaking into his own tears while staring at this new little member of the family. "Thank you, Jesus, for our little girl, Stephanie!"

Betty couldn't wait to get off work. Kim had just called. She and Tom were home with Stephanie. "I've just got to get over there and see my new granddaughter," she thought. The dedicated, hard-working accountant got up from her desk and walked into her boss' office. He looked up from the stack of papers he had been reviewing. "I have to go," she told him. "My daughter and son-in-law just brought home their new baby girl!"

Her boss just stared at her, not saying a word. Then he looked back at his charts. Betty left the room. She waited a few minutes, and still there was no approval, so she went back down the hall and entered her boss' office again. The reply this time was different. He looked at her and told her he would let her know as soon as he could.

That reply upset the grandmother's apple cart. She walked back to her desk, put away everything on her desk, and stopped by his office on her way out of the building. He looked up. "I'll be back tomorrow. This is my new granddaughter, and I'm going to go see her." The man gave her a penetrating glare, but at this point it didn't matter to her. In just a little while, she would be holding her daughter's precious infant in her arms.

Forty-five minutes later, Betty sat on the couch holding her new granddaughter. What a happy day it was! From the time Kim was young, her mother had talked to her about adoption, worried that somehow those conversations would impact Kim in a negative way. Now she was holding the little girl Kim had talked about when she was young.

Stephanie's whimper was barely audible, but the engrossed grandmother was holding the infant so close to her that she heard her right away. Suspecting what might be making her cry, she called out to Kim. "May I change her diaper?" she asked.

"Sure. Everything you'll need is near her crib, including the diapers, ointment, and wipes."

Betty carried her new granddaughter into the beautifully decorated nursery, laid her in the crib, and started to remove the infant's diaper. "Stephanie!" Kim heard the call from the other end of the house. The new mother went to see what was happening. Betty looked up when she heard Kim approach and giggled. "You've got a live wire here! I take the afternoon off from work, drive all the way here, and hold Stephanie for just a few minutes. Look what she gave me in return—a wet sleeve!" The humored grandmother finished changing her grand-daughter's diaper, washed off her arm and hands, picked the tiny girl up from her crib, and gave her a big hug. "I love you anyway, you little stinker," Betty whis-pered affectionately, placing a kiss on the tiny girl's forehead.

Chapter Twenty-Four

Motherhood was a dream come true for Kim. She and Tom loved their daughter so much that they wanted to spend every waking moment with her. Tom was working nights, so he could enjoy getting to know his little girl during the day. Kim quit her job at Pepsi to stay home.

For the first eighteen months of Stephanie's life, Kim took on little jobs to help out with the bills. She wanted to stay home as long as she could with the precious bundle the Lord had given them. She did in-home child care, sold Tupperware, started an in-home makeup sales business, and even did short-term projects at Pepsi. But after a few months, it was obvious she needed to go back to work and bring home a steady income. Looking through the newspaper one evening, she found a full-time job at a yogurt shop. She applied and went for an interview the next day. She was hired the following day and went to work immediately. Within one month she moved up to a management position. She liked that she could make her own schedule so she could be home with Stephanie when Tom was at work.

As Kim's six-month anniversary of working for the yogurt company approached, her supervisor called her about a possible promotion to division manager. Mr. Richardson, the franchisee of the yogurt stores, was sending a couple store managers to the home office to work as division managers. Division managers would go out in the field to assist franchisees in opening new stores, get store budgets in place, and maintain company standards. Kim was chosen to be one of the division managers.

The following week Kim was sitting in Mr. Richardson's office lobby waiting to talk to him. "Kim, please come in," he said, as he stepped through the door and welcomed her into his office.

The franchisee began by explaining in more detail the division manager's responsibilities and the salary and benefit package they were offering. The young woman was amazed at the opportunity. She wanted to accept immediately, but she knew she needed to discuss it with her husband. "I'll have to talk this over with my husband," she told the owner, "and I'll get back with you soon."

"Great!" Mr. Richardson expressed his appreciation. "Now, I'd like to get an idea where you would like to live if you take the position."

"What are my options?" Kim asked.

"Pretty much anywhere in the United States," he replied. "We are just starting the hiring program, so you can go almost anywhere."

"Okay, then my first choice would be Detroit."

Mr. Richardson shook his head, thinking he had not heard her correctly. "Excuse me," he said, implying that he needed her to repeat herself.

"Detroit," she confirmed.

"Detroit?" This time he knew he had heard her correctly, but he had no idea why someone would want to live there. "You mean somewhere in the Detroit area, like Ann Arbor?"

"No. I mean Detroit proper. My father recently accepted a call to be the minister at the same church we attended in Detroit when I was a child. He and my mother moved there three months ago. My daughter, Stephanie, would be able to live near at least one set of grandparents. My husband's father is a job shopper. He and Tom's mother move quite a bit. Living in Detroit will be perfect. The parochial grade school Stephanie would go to is the same one I attended as a child."

Mr. Richardson still seemed confused, but he moved his head up and down in understanding. "Okay," he said hesitantly. "Well, as soon as you and your husband make a decision, please let me know. We will need to schedule your three weeks of training at the home office."

The man's last statement threw Kim for a small loop. "Three weeks?" she asked.

"Yes. You do three weeks of training. They'll set you up with your benefits package, an expense account, and a new company car."

Kim was exasperated and quite overwhelmed. God was very gracious to her!

Tom was home from work by the time Kim got back from her interview. "How'd it go?" he asked.

"Fine, but you are not going to believe what happened. They want me to be a division manager for the company."

This brought Tom's attention from his current task to listen carefully to his wife's words. Kim paused to watch Tom's face.

"Wow! And...?" Tom saw hesitation in her eyes, and he knew his wife's facial expressions enough to know that he did not yet have all the information.

"And...we would have to move."

"And…?" This is like pulling teeth, Tom thought.

"And I would have to go to the home office for three weeks of training."

Now that he had all the news, he also had questions. "Where would we have to move to?" he began his line of interrogation.

"Anywhere in the United States. I told Mr. Richardson we would talk about it and get back with him. If I do this, though, you will have to be a stay-at-home dad while I'm in training and until we get settled in our house."

"That's not a problem, but have you thought about where we should live?"

"Yes, and there is only one place that makes sense—Detroit. Now that my parents live there, Stephanie could grow up around at least one set of her grandparents. With the type of job your father has, your parents never know where they are going next. If we go to Detroit, Stephanie would have at least one set of grandparents nearby, and she would be able to attend the Lutheran day school where I went."

Tom weighed all of Kim's words. Giving Stephanie a Christian education was important to both of them. For her to get to go to the same school where Kim went from third through sixth grade was kind of neat. "Honey, I think we should do it," he said. "It is a great opportunity for you, and being in the hotel business, I will be able to transfer easily. I'll talk to my manager tomorrow."

Kim hugged Tom in response. "That's a good idea. We should probably think about it for a day or two anyway."

A week later, Kim met with Mr. Richardson to accept the promotion.

That night when she got home, she called her parents. "Hello," her mother answered after the phone had rung only once.

"Hi, Mom. How are you?"

"I'm fine. How are you?"

"I'm fine, and I have some great news. Can Dad get on the phone?" Kim wanted to share the news with both parents at the same time.

"I'm on the other extension," her dad answered.

"Guess what?" Kim could hardly wait to tell them, but she also enjoyed drawing the surprise out as long as possible.

"What?" They both pushed for the news.

"I got a promotion today!" Kim informed them.

"That's great!" Both of her parents were excited for her.

"Now do you want the good news?" Kim antagonized them one more time.

"That sounded like good news," her father stated.

"Oh, but this news will make you even more excited." Kim paused for one last time. "We're moving to Detroit."

"*What?*" her mother shouted.

"We're moving to Detroit, and I am going to be the division manager for Michigan."

Betty could hardly believe her ears. She started to cry. "I sure have missed you kids since we have been up here. This is an answer to prayer!"

Kim went on to explain the plan to both of her parents. They were so thrilled. Five weeks later Tom and Stephanie were on their way to Detroit to find a house, and Kim had finished her first week of training for division manager.

Chapter Twenty-Five

Tom, Kim, and Stephanie settled into life in Detroit very easily. Tom secured a job with a storage company, Kim began visiting with her new franchisees, and Stephanie became friends with the children at church rather quickly. She also enjoyed time with her grandparents. They took her places and had her and her friends over to spend the night on occasion. Ah! Life was finally becoming normal again just in time for Stephanie to start school.

Tom got up early that morning. "Honey," he said, rolling over to wake Kim up. "Stephanie should be getting up soon. I'm going to make her some pancakes while she gets ready."

Kim slowly opened her eyes. "Okay. I'll get her up and dressed. Are you going with us to school?"

"Of course, I am. It's her first day. I can't miss out on that." Tom glowed with that "she's daddy's little girl" grin that so often covered his face. "And let's not forget to take her picture on the way out the door."

"Right."

By 8:30 AM breakfast was eaten, pictures were taken, and Stephanie was delivered to her kindergarten classroom. Tom and Kim left the school with the sad knowledge that another "apron string" had been cut.

Kim's role as mother and wife could not have been more precious. Stephanie loved her school. The fact that her nana and papa lived next door and she got to see them often was wonderful. Tom and Kim had a great time watching their daughter grow. They participated in all of the school functions possible and spent quite a bit of time with Kim's parents.

About three and a half years into this settled life, Kim noticed that her stamina was changing. She was getting tired more easily. At first she tried slowing down by getting a later start to the day. Then she needed to rest midafternoon. Finally she mentioned it to her husband.

She woke up late one morning, and Tom had not left for work yet. "Tom, I'm not feeling well. Can you please call my boss and let him know that I won't be working today?"

"Sure. Are you okay?"

"I think so. I can't seem to get up enough energy to get out of bed. Has Stephanie left for school yet?"

"Yes. Her ride came a little early today. Do you think you should go to the doctor?"

"I'm going to take off from work today and see if that helps. If I'm not feeling better by the end of the week, then I can make an appointment. Quite frankly, I feel the same way I did when I had endocarditis. This is not a good thing."

Two days passed with no change and Kim decided a doctor's visit was necessary. She had little energy. Friday Kim called her boss when she got home from the doctor's office. The phone rang several times before he answered.

"Hello?" his voice rang out over the receiver.

"Hi, Allan. How are you?" Kim inquired.

"I'm fine, but how are you? Are you getting rested up?"

"I went to the doctor today because my low energy level is not improving. He says he thinks I may have mononucleosis. I can't seem to shake the fatigue. Getting out of bed is even a chore at times. My physician wants me to take four weeks off to rest. He is hoping I am just worn-out."

The man on the other end of the phone sounded somewhat frustrated, yet sympathetic. "Well, okay. Take care of yourself, and I'll call you again soon to find out how you are doing."

"I can take phone calls if you need me to." Kim tried to help. "That's something I can do from the couch."

"No. Rest and get better. There is a lot of work to do in your territory."

"All right."

Kim knew she had been working too hard and pushing her limits. Part of her job required long days and physical labor. She had run herself down so far that she wasn't sure she could recover.

After seven weeks of rest, Kim's health did not improve the way the doctor thought it would. In fact, her symptoms were getting worse. Worry started to set into Kim's mind. Maybe she had endocarditis again. No. If that was it, she would be in the hospital by now. The symptoms she had and those of endocarditis were very much alike, but not exactly the same. Of course, these thoughts made her worry even more. She had a job to do and a family to take care of. She did not have time for a bout of endocarditis. Then her thoughts progressed into fear. What if something was going wrong with her heart? Hadn't the cardiologists said there was more surgery in her future? In the back of her mind, even the thought of an early death lingered as it had for many years. Stop, she told herself. Don't let the frustration of not knowing get the best of you. Do something.

Taking her own advice, Kim called a local cardiologist. Through her years in Michigan, she had been traveling down to Atlanta to Emory University for her checkups. She didn't feel that trip was warranted, as she had just been there four months prior. This time she would go to a local cardiologist. If her illness was something serious, she would make the trip to Atlanta, but that would be a last resort.

Carrying her medical reports from her family doctor under her arm, she and her husband walked into the local cardiologist's office. "I'm here to see Dr. Riley," Kim told the woman behind the desk.

"Please have a seat, and we will be with you shortly," the receptionist replied in a somewhat mechanical voice.

Kim and Tom sat and waited. When the nurse called Kimberly to the back, Tom sat in the waiting room. "If I need you, I'll have them get you," Tom's nervous wife called out over her shoulder.

Tom sat patiently waiting.

The exam room was much the same as all the others. It was small, with equipment tightly fit into every corner and several neatly displayed documents hanging on the walls. Kim was looking at each one, trying to get a better idea of the education and interests of this cardiologist. As she gazed from picture frame to picture frame, the words *very impressive* crossed her mind. Then her eyes fell on one that got her full attention. She scanned all the words in print, both large and small, on the disturbing certificate. Two words struck her: Heart Transplant. This cardiologist was a member of a heart transplant organization. Oh, my!

There was a slight rap on the door, and the doctor came in. He reached to shake her hand. "My name is Dr. Riley," he began his introduction. "I glanced over your chart. Tell me what brings you here today."

"I've been feeling run-down, my body aches, and my energy is pretty much nonexistent. It has been this way for about three months now. My family physician thought I had mononucleosis, but the symptoms are not going away. They are getting worse. I need help. I can't keep going like this." Tears appeared in Kim's soft blue eyes, and one slowly rolled down her cheek.

"I see," the doctor paused thoughtfully. "Let me listen to your heart." After listening carefully to each necessary place on Kim's chest and back, the cardiologist leaned against a cabinet. "That is some rattle you heart is making. Have you had a checkup recently?"

"No. Not since last year."

The doctor smugly stared at the floor. "Has it occurred to you that you might be in the throes of heart failure?"

Heart failure? Of course, she had not thought about that.

Kim had an uneasy feeling about what was transpiring, but she gave the doctor a chance to finish his explanation. "Here are a couple prescriptions," he said, handing her two small sheets of paper. "One is for blood work, and one is for a nuclear test. This test is like an echocardiogram, but we insert dye into your veins and watch the directions of your blood flow. When you have the results of both of these, come back and see me."

One week later the test results were in, and Kim was back in the cardiologist's office. The doctor knocked on the door, then opened it, and slowly entered.

He hesitated before beginning. "Your tests have confirmed my thoughts, Kim. You are in the beginning stages of heart failure."

Kim sucked in a deep breath. She knew what his next words would be.

"Do you have any children?"

"Yes, one daughter."

"How old is she?"

"She's nine."

The doctor couldn't look Kim in the face with his next words. It was as if his eyes were glued in a downward position. "Nine. Hmm. Kim, your heart failure is serious enough that we need to begin considering a heart transplant. I use the words *begin considering,* because we don't do transplants on women with children under the age of eleven."

The image of the document Kim had noticed during her first appointment flashed before her. "What? Have you read *all* of my chart? Did you carefully review the heart surgeries I've already had?"

The cardiologist looked up at her. He had never had a patient talk so sternly to him. Most patients listened, took time to think about his recommendations, and made the decision about what to do. This lady was drilling him.

"Did you carefully review the heart surgeries I've already had?" Kim repeated.

"Well, I saw that you have a congenital defect."

"And did you read all of the records?" The more questions she asked, the more livid she became.

"Enough to know what is going on." Dr. Riley started to become defensive.

"What do you know about congenital heart defects?"

"I learned a little about them in med school," he defended himself.

"How many cases have you actually taken care of?" The thirty-two-year-old patient was not backing down. This situation was ridiculous. How many patients have come through this office and not had enough knowledge to question what this doctor told them, Kim wondered.

"I haven't taken care of any," the doctor confessed.

"Have you conferred with someone who has, someone who has experience in congenital heart defects?"

"No." The doctor became uncomfortable with the line of questioning.

"How can you just make a rash decision about something so serious? You barely read my chart. You listened to a few sounds in my chest and read the results of a few tests. Then you quickly concluded that I need a heart transplant."

"Kim, news like this is not easy. I realize that. Why don't you take some time to think about it, and when you are more comfortable talking about it, you can come back?"

Kim got up from her place on the exam table. She was so upset and angry that she was shaking and teary-eyed. "If you had really researched my case, you would have realized that so much of my blood has been rerouted that a transplant is not even an option for me. And as far as the Doppler test you prescribed, apparently the technicians didn't read my charts either, because they spent forty-five minutes searching for the septum between my ventricles when I only have one to begin with. Thank you for your services, but I am no longer interested." With that she marched quickly from the room and out to the lobby where her husband waited, tears flooding her cheeks.

Chapter Twenty-Six

"You know, if we had not already planned a vacation to Atlanta, I would not have agreed to go and see Dr. Franch," Kim told her husband as they drove south on I-75 toward Georgia. "I think that I am feeling a little better."

"Kim, you ride in a wheelchair whenever we have to walk at the mall or anywhere else that is a considerable distance. A wheelchair! That is not a good thing! Let Dr. Franch evaluate your health, and let's see what he has to say. If he doesn't think we need to worry, we won't, but you need to let the cardiologists decide what is best. They are the ones who are trained in heart medicine." Tom spoke uncompromisingly to his wife. She knew he was right. At the same time, it seemed like a lot of bother when Kim thought she was starting to feel better.

Two days later Tom and Kim sat in Dr. Franch's office waiting for him to return with her test results. They were only there a few minutes when he strolled through the doorway carrying the patient's medical chart. "Good morning," he greeted them both. After sitting down at his desk, he looked through Kim's test results one last time.

Looking up, he sat back in his chair and began. "I've looked through your medical reports from the last six months and compared them to the results of the tests we ran yesterday. It is quite apparent that your oxygen level is declining." Kim tuned him out for a short time. This was not what she wanted to hear, and the face of the cardiologist who told her she needed a heart transplant flashed through her mind.

"But I feel as though I might be getting better," Kim began to argue, knowing full well that the doctor's words were heading in a direction she wanted to avoid.

"Today, even, you are in a wheelchair, Kim. The pulse/oxygen machine does not lie. It shows your oxygen level is down to 79 percent. Because of your condition, we don't expect 97 to 100 percent like a healthy person, but 79 percent is very low. We need to find out what is causing your trouble." He went on with a little more explanation. "The heart catheterization from yesterday brings me to the conclusion that you should probably go to Mayo Clinic, like you did last time. I will get you an appointment with Dr. Carole Warnes, who is one of the best congenital heart doctors around, and Mayo Clinic has all the state-of-the-art equipment to assist her in evaluating your situation."

Kim felt her illness was getting blown way out of proportion. She was not that sick. There was no way that some sort of treatment, possibly even surgery, was warranted. At the same time, she knew that Dr. Franch had no reason to ask this of her if it was not necessary. As uneasy as she was with the entire turn of events, she knew the trip to Mayo was inevitable.

Two months later, in October, Dr. Carole Warnes entered the exam room and introduced herself to Tom and Kim. Her cheerfulness and sincerity won Tom and Kim's confidence immediately. The fact that she loved helping people was very evident. "So tell me a little bit about what has been going on," she said, as she smoothed her skirt and sat in the rolling chair in front of the desk.

Kim explained her decline in health over the last several months. Tom helped fill in the details as she talked.

Dr. Warnes took notes as they described Kim's symptoms. When they were done speaking, she expressed her thoughts in her beautiful English accent. "Well, the results from the X rays, echocardiogram, and blood work done earlier today leave me with a few questions. Your oxygen level has definitely declined. The echocardiogram revealed some helpful information but not enough for us to determine exactly what is going on. I would like to admit you to the hospital and do a heart catheterization tomorrow morning."

Yet again, Kim found herself in tears. "So you think it *is* heart related?"

Dr. Warnes shrugged her shoulders. "It is a suspicion, but I do not have enough solid evidence. The solid evidence comes from a heart cath."

As much as Kim had not wanted to hear this news, she surrendered to the cardiologist that dear Dr. Franch had recommended. "Okay," she conceded. "What do we need to do from here?"

Dr. Warnes explained where to be admitted and what to expect after the heart catheterization the following day.

The next afternoon Kim was released from the hospital early enough to arrange a late appointment with Dr. Warnes. She walked into the comfortable office, accompanied by one of the surgeons on staff, Dr. David Andrews. Tom and Kim shook hands with both cardiologists. Kim and Tom sat down on the comfortable leather couch, Dr. Warnes sat in her rolling chair as usual, and Dr. Andrews stood. "How did it go this morning?" Dr. Warnes addressed her new patient.

"Fine. I almost backed out at the last minute. I always get so scared."

Dr. Warnes put on her pleasant smile. "Yes, I heard you tried to talk the technician into taking you back to your room. They called us to find out what to do."

"Oh," Kim said in embarrassment. "They said you would come down if I needed you to. That's when I realized the procedure was really important. They gave me some medicine. After that I didn't care much about anything."

Dr. Warnes grinned and redirected the conversation. "This is Dr. Andrews, who is one of our cardiac surgeons." Immediately Kim tensed up. "He and I have reviewed the results of your tests and catheterization, which show that your Blalock-Taussig shunts from the 1960s are no longer providing you with the amount of blood flow you need for proper oxygenation."

Kim took in a deep breath. This can't be happening, she thought. I have lived for thirty-two years because of those two shunts. They are my lifelines. She snapped out of her deep thoughts, realizing she needed to know the plan that the surgeon and cardiologist had made.

Dr. Andrews spoke first. "After doing some research and talking to some other cardiologists and surgeons, we conclude that there is a surgery that will increase your oxygen level and in turn improve your health."

All of Kim's built-up stress released itself in the form of tears. Sobs came from her innermost being; she bawled so hard that her body shook. Part of her felt glad to finally get firm medical advice, and the other part was scared to death. Through all of her years, an early death had been in the back of her mind. The reality that it might come soon terrified her. She knew she would have eternal life in heaven because Jesus came to earth to earn that for her. What bothered her was the actual act of dying and leaving her family behind.

"Kim," Dr. Andrews said, trying to get the patient's attention again. "All we want to do is add a third shunt to assist the two you already have. It is called a Glenn shunt. A small tube will connect your ascending aorta to the left main pulmonary artery."

Keep the old ones and add a new one? Kim contemplated whether this was a good idea. At least she would get to keep the Blalock-Taussig shunts that enabled her to live for so many years. "Does this really need to be done soon? I'm not sure I feel bad enough to justify having surgery." Kim was trying to talk her way out of the inevitable.

Dr. Warnes leaned forward and looked directly at Kim. "You are in a wheelchair, Kim. Would you be if you didn't *have* to be?"

That was the question that brought Kim to the reality of her condition. She always used any energy she had to its fullest. The wheelchair was a necessity to her right now. "No," she admitted.

"Then let's set December first as the date for surgery," Dr. Warnes said reassuringly.

"How long will I have to be hospitalized?" Kim asked reluctantly.

"Five to seven days," Dr. Andrews said softly. Even though he had performed many cardiac surgeries, this talk with his patients always tugged at his emotions.

He adjusted his tie, reached over and patted Kim on the shoulder, and looked reassuringly into her eyes. "I feel confident about this." His words were greatly appreciated, but they did not bring much comfort.

In preparation for her upcoming surgery, Kim took extra measures to make sure things were in order at home. She had two months to prepare her house and her family. She began by training Stephanie in the areas of cleaning, cooking, and laundry. In the back of her mind, she knew part of her drive was to make sure that Stephanie could help her father run the house if something happened to her during surgery. She wanted to know that her family would be able to function without her.

Kim also bought and wrapped all of the family's Christmas gifts. When she and her family went to Georgia to visit in November, they delivered the presents. Reviewing the list she had made, she realized she had accomplished everything that needed to be done.

Chapter Twenty-Seven

On November 30, 1992, the evening before Kim's anticipated heart surgery, Tom and Kim met with the surgeon and cardiologist one last time. The surgeon came into the office where they were waiting and addressed both of them. "Are you ready for tomorrow?" Dr. Andrews spoke softly to his patient and her husband.

"Yes, I guess so," the thirty-two-year-old woman replied timidly.

"We have a change of plans with your surgery," the surgeon began. "Because your Blalock-Taussig shunts are working minimally, they need to be tied off. So during surgery we will take them down, put in one central shunt, and connect a vein from your neck next to it. The old shunts are not benefiting you in any way. We don't want to leave them up, because they could cause complications later.

"Keeping your old shunts and adding the new shunt might increase your pressures so much that your arteries cannot tolerate it. For the central shunt, we will place a seven-millimeter piece of tubing from the ascending aorta to the left pulmonary artery. Knowing exactly what size of tube your blood is flowing through will help us determine the amount of oxygen you are getting."

How much more could Kim take? And the night before surgery! Tom held her as she let out her sobs. "I've lived on those shunts for thirty-two years and you are going to take them down? I need them."

Dr. Andrews understood Kim's feelings and concerns. "The new shunt will take their place and be more effective," he reassured her. "Connecting a vein from your neck to your pulmonary artery next to it will ensure that the pulmonary artery pressure does not get too high. If necessary, the blood will go up into the neck artery to relieve the pressure.

"Usually the insertion of the central shunt and relocation of the super vena cava are done in two different operations. I have never done them both at the same time, but I've looked over your pulmonary anatomy, and I am confident that I can get to both sites through one incision."

Kim bawled outright. She was overwhelmed. First they were going to take down the shunts she had had all her life, and now they planned to do a surgery that had never been done before. Dr. Andrews gave her time to absorb the initial shock. "Kim, we have done both surgeries several times. If I can open you once and do it all, wouldn't that be to everyone's advantage?"

Tom reached over, patted Kim's hand, and held it tightly. "It's going to be okay, Dear. The Lord Jesus is our refuge and strength, remember?" Those words didn't take all the pain away, but Kim knew it was true. That evening she was admitted to the hospital for her 7:00 AM surgery the next morning.

The weather was cold and windy, with snow blowing in every which way in typical Minnesota style. Tom, Stephanie, Tom's sister Peggy, and Kim's parents made their way across the busy road to St. Mary's Hospital. It was rather early in the morning, but they wanted to visit with Kim before surgery. A petite, red-headed nurse came in around 6:45 AM to announce that there was a delay, and Kim would not be going to the operating room until around 10:00 AM.

Nine-thirty rolled around, and the same nurse brought medication to calm Kim's anxiety. "This will help you relax," the nurse addressed her. "Someone from the surgical team should be here to get you in just a little bit."

Kim's minister/father gathered everyone around the bed for prayer. "Lord, bless this child of yours during this operation. You are the Great Physician, Lord Jesus. Bless the doctors, nurses, and medical staff, guiding them each step of the way according to your will. Bless Kim with good health and healing, that she may return home and serve you all of her days. We ask this for Jesus' sake, in whose name we further pray. Our Father, who art in heaven, hallowed be thy name, thy kingdom come, thy will be done on earth as it is in heaven. Give us this day our daily bread; and forgive us our trespasses, as we forgive those who trespass against us; and lead us not into temptation, but deliver us from evil. For thine is the kingdom and the power and the glory forever and ever. Amen."

Water droplets had left Kim's eyes and landed on her pillow as the prayer ended. She knew she was strong enough to do this with God by her side.

A man in a blue paper hat, clothes, and shoe covers came through the door. "Kimberly Russell?" He checked the patient's plastic bracelet to make sure he had the right patient. Kim nodded in confirmation. "Are you ready to go?" he inquired.

"Yes," the hesitant young woman answered nervously.

The worker began preparing Kim's hospital bed for the trip to the operating room as he addressed the family. "We are taking her to the operating holding area now. You may go to the surgical waiting area. A nurse will be waiting there for you."

As the transporter began pushing Kim's bed, her father leaned over to give her one last blessing. Then her mother kissed her, whispering loving words close to her ear. After that, Tom leaned over her and whispered sweet nothings into her ear, reminding her that he loved her very much. He reached down and picked up their daughter, Stephanie, so she could give her mother a kiss. "I love you, Mama," the ten-year-old girl told her mother, giving her one last hug.

"I love you too, Sweetheart! I'll see you later." Kim was trying to be strong, but on the inside her fears were playing havoc with her nerves. The medication calmed her some, but the pain of leaving her family, knowing that she might not see them again this side of heaven, was incredible.

Kim's family members arrived in the surgical waiting area a short time later. "Hi," the nurse greeted them as they walked through the doorway. "My name is Carolyn. We will be spending time together over the next few hours. Some call me the operating room reporter, because that is what I do. I'll keep you updated as things progress in the operating room. I'll tell you when the operation begins and when Kimberly is on the heart-lung bypass machine. I'll report one time during the actual surgerical repair, as soon as she is off the heart-lung machine, and when she has been taken to the surgical recovery room." The whole family was thankful that they would get detailed information about their loved-one's progress.

Carolyn walked to the other side of the room. "Here are the snack and pop machines. There is coffee right here on this table. Feel free to go out for lunch or whatever you want to do. The surgery will take about four to six hours. If you are not here when I come to report, I'll come again soon."

Tom, Peggy, Larry, and Betty all agreed that someone would always be in the waiting area in case they were needed.

Lying on the gurney, Kim contemplated calling the whole thing off. She could just get dressed, go home, and enjoy what health she had. But the man pushing her through hallway after hallway talked to her constantly to keep her distracted.

Arriving in the patient waiting area, the transporter parked Kim's bed against the wall. "How are you?" he asked. Kim could not hold back any longer. She stayed quiet, but tears gushed from her eyes. "I'll let the surgical team know you are here. Maybe they can give you more medicine." Kim gave him a knowing glance but didn't say a word.

Time passed slowly for Kim's relatives. They talked, tried to keep Stephanie entertained, and ate lunch. True to her word, Carolyn came at the proper intervals to let them know the surgery was going smoothly. "Good news," she reported the first time. "The operation has begun, and Kim is doing well. She was very nervous, but with medication she finally relaxed."

"Thank you," Tom replied. He appreciated the nurse's announcement. Everyone smiled, glad for the report, but the announcement they were looking forward to would not come for another five hours.

Report after report came with no worrisome information. Kimberly was put on bypass and taken off with no unnatural events. Everyone was relieved to hear that all had gone well.

The next report came from Dr. Andrews. "The surgery was a great success. The shunt we put in is working and has already increased her oxygen level. We used a seven-millimeter piece of tubing for the central shunt, and the blood is flowing well through it. The neck vein that we connected to the pulmonary artery next to it is also flowing to full capacity. Kim will be in the recovery area for a couple hours. You can see her later when they bring her to the intensive care unit. She should feel much better in a few days."

The family members hugged and smiled, glad that the hardest part of Kim's hospital stay was over. Larry led a prayer of thanksgiving.

Chapter Twenty-Eight

Dr. Andrews smiled when he approached Kim's bedside two days after surgery. "We did it!" he confirmed. "Two operations in one. How do you feel?"

"I'm okay. I'll be glad to get rid of all these tubes, especially Irving." Kim gave the doctor a smirk.

The doctor turned his head sideways in confusion. "Irving?"

"Yes. That's what I named my first IV pole. The name has stuck with him all these years."

The doctor chuckled. Then he noticed several glasses and juice containers lining Kim's bed tray. Frowning slightly, he asked, "Are all of those yours, or is your husband the thirsty one?"

"They're mine," Kim said proudly. "I am trying to drink as much as I can to flush out the anesthetic and dye." She was so pleased with herself about knowing what to do. She did not understand why he was looking at her like this.

He stood tall as he looked down at her. "You are now on a new medication to help get rid of excess fluids. Drinking that much will defeat the purpose."

Kim shrunk into her covers. "Oh" was all she could say in a timid voice. The surgeon smiled. "You can drink, just not that much," he advised her. "Your chest and stomach tubes will be taken out the day after tomorrow. Dr. Warnes will be coming by every day. If all continues to go well, you can go home by the beginning of next week. Dr. Warnes will make out your release papers. I'll see you when you come back for your three-month checkup." With that he turned and walked out the door, grinning from ear to ear.

Three hours later Dr. Warnes came in to check on her young heart patient. "How are you?" she inquired, lifting the covers to check Kim's foot color and swollen ankles. The cardiologist tapped her toes. "Uncross those legs, young lady. We don't need a blood clot to complicate things." Kim obeyed immediately.

"You sure look good," the attentive doctor announced.

"I feel so weak," Kim said with concern.

"Have you been getting up?" Dr. Warnes asked.

"Yes. I sat in the chair a couple times this morning, but it is so much work to get in and out of bed," Kim reported.

"How is your appetite?" the cardiologist inquired.

"I am not hungry, but I'm drinking enough to stay hydrated."

"Good," Dr. Warnes stated as she began listening to Kim's chest and back. "It sounds as though the shunt is working well. Let's give it a few days and see how you do."

Day by day Kim's strength returned. She was too weak to go home in the predicted seven-day period, but by the end of ten days she was released to make the long trip home to Michigan.

The car trip home was somewhat unbearable for Kim. She was still weak and tired, and every bump and turn jarred her healing sternum, which caused her ribs to rub against each other. Tom and Betty took turns driving. Larry had already gone home. Stephanie slept quietly in the back as usual. She had always been a good traveler, as she loved to sleep in the car.

Halfway through the six-hundred-mile trip home, the group decided to stop and spend the night. Kim appreciated that very much. She felt horrible. Her head ached and her back hurt. She started throwing up. Tom and Betty weren't sure what to do. Was this normal, or did Kim need medical attention.

Tom took charge of the situation. "Let's ride it out for a while and see how she does. If she's not better in a couple hours, we'll call Mayo." But after taking a hot bath and her pain medication, Kim was able to sleep well. They did not plan to get up at any specific time; they would allow Kim to get as much rest as needed. By ten o'clock the next morning they were back on the road.

They had been home for only a few days when Kim noticed that Tom had a bad cough. "Honey, do you need to see the doctor about that? You've had it for quite a few days."

In normal male style, Tom replied, "No, I'm fine."

Three days later he was still coughing. "Tom, you really need to go to the doctor. That cough is sounding worse." Kim was getting more and more concerned.

"It'll be okay," Tom stated "Don't worry so much."

Finally after two more days, Kim picked up the phone and made Tom an appointment with the family physician. When Tom came home from work early that day, she was glad she had. "Here is your appointment for tomorrow morning at 9 AM," Kim said as Tom stretched out on the loveseat.

Tom frowned but knew his wife was right. It was time to do something.

At eleven o'clock the next morning, Tom called from the doctor's office. "I am being admitted into the hospital," he huffed mildly. "The doctor says I have pneumonia."

Kim's heart nearly stopped. "Are you going to be okay?"

"Yes. He wants me to have three days of intravenous antibiotics."

Kim felt horrible. Here she was lying on the couch unable to do much at all, let alone drive. "I'm so sorry, Dear! What can I do?"

"Call your parents and let them know. Maybe someone could come and bring you here." It was the only thing he could think to do. In the meantime, Kim dreaded the thought of getting dressed and leaving home.

"Okay. I'll be there as soon as I can. Honey, are you okay?"

"I'll be fine, but please come as soon as you can."

As soon as they hung up, Kim called her mother and explained the situation. "I can come and take you there. I'll have Dad bring Stephanie home from school. She can stay with us until Tom gets out of the hospital." Kim's mother was anxious to help.

"That would be great. Thanks, Mom." Kim's stress was relieved immediately.

"I'll be over as soon as I can."

Two hours later Betty and Kim were walking through the door of the hospital in search of Tom. He was already checked in and getting settled in his room.

When Kim and Betty arrived at his room, the door was shut. Tom was getting dressed in a fashionable hospital gown. When the door opened, the two women entered, each giving him a needed hug. Kim handed him the bag of items she thought he might need.

"How do you feel?" Kim asked him.

"Not that bad. I was very surprised when the doctor said pneumonia. The more I think about it though, the more I realize how short of breath I was getting." Tom gave them an account of what activities made him know that a doctor's visit was necessary.

After an hour Kim was getting tired. She needed to go home and lie on the couch. She looked at Tom as if she was about to betray him. He was always so good to her when she was sick, especially during her recent recovery from surgery, but she needed to go home. "Honey, I'm sorry to make this visit short, but I am exhausted. I need to go home and lie down."

In true Tom Russell fashion, he understood and agreed, even though he really wanted her to stay with him. "When will you be back?" he wanted to know.

"As soon as I can get someone to bring me," she assured him and kissed him on the forehead instead of the mouth to keep from being infected. They held hands for a short time before Kim and Betty left.

Tom's hospital stay seemed to last forever. Kim's exhaustion prevented her from seeing him as much as she wanted. In fact, she only went back one more time. The couple visited over the phone for long periods of time. They were very glad when Tom was released and the whole family was back at home together.

Kim's recovery took longer than expected. She was so weak before surgery that her body just didn't have the strength to heal quickly. Sometimes she got the feeling that she would never recover enough to go back to her full-time job and live a normal life. Eventually her Mayo Clinic cardiologist explained to her that she would probably not be released to go back to work.

Kim was torn about this. First of all, she had loved her job. Second, it meant admitting that she was really "sick." Third, it left her future hanging in the balance. How much better would she get? Would she ever go back to work? Kim's family reminded her that her Lord was in control and had a plan for her. "He'll use you in a special way," her husband encouraged.

Knowing Tom was right, Kim took the opportunity to get more involved in Stephanie's school. She helped organize fund-raisers, taught beginning computer to the younger students two hours a week, joined the Monday morning Bible study for women, and became a youth leader with Tom for the seventh- and eighth-grade group at church. She also joined the Women's Mission Society. It was just enough activity to keep her busy, yet she was able to rest as much as she needed.

One afternoon while Kim was home finishing the paperwork for a recent fund-raiser, Stephanie came bursting through the door from school. "Mom, guess what?"

Kim stood up from her chair and went to meet her. "What, honey? What?" The loving mother leaned over to hug her daughter.

"Mom, Miss Martin told us the title of the play we are doing this year. Guess what it is." Stephanie could not get the words out fast enough.

"I have no idea," Kim said, trying to think about what it might be.

"The Pirates of Penzance!" Stephanie said as she broke into her mother's concentration. *"The Pirates of Penzance.* Just like you were in, Mom. Isn't that cool?"

Kim reached down and hugged her daughter in excitement. "That's great! Did she give you your parts?"

"No," Stephanie answered, looking down as if frustrated. "We won't know for three more weeks."

"That's not too long from now," her mother replied, patting her on the back to assure her the time would pass quickly.

The projected three weeks did not go fast enough for Stephanie. Day after day passed slowly until finally, early one morning, right after the Pledge of Allegiance, Miss Martin announced who had what part in the play.

When Stephanie got in the car that afternoon, a wide smile spread across her face. "Mom, we found out today! We got our parts for *The Pirates of Penzance.*"

"You did? And…?" Kim waited patiently for the news.

"And I got a part as a policeman, just like you did. I am the *lead* policeman." Stephanie looked at her mom, knowing she would be thrilled.

"Wow! That's great! You got the same part I had. That is neat."

"Well, it's not for eight more weeks," Stephanie informed her mother. "But we are going to start playing softball soon too. That should be fun."

"Who are you playing ball with?" Kim inquired.

"The third through eighth graders are being mixed into two teams, and we will be playing against each other."

"That's a neat idea," Kim commented. "Where will you play?"

"There is a field about six blocks from school. We are going to walk over there after school to practice."

"Great!"

Between softball games and play practices, spring arrived rather quickly, and so did the operetta, *The Pirates of Penzance.* Kim was as excited as Stephanie, if not more so.

Kim, Tom, and Kim's parents all attended. Larry had to stand in the back of the auditorium, though, to help supervise the event. Everyone else arrived early to get good seats. After they had been sitting for about thirty minutes, the lights flashed to signal the beginning of the play.

The school children were well prepared! They executed each line and song with good diction and precision. Kim sat in her seat having a great time singing to herself all of the songs she had memorized years ago. Tom sat proudly and in awe of how much material the children had learned. Betty sat next to them taking it all in.

At the beginning of the second half, Larry stood next to the back door as Stephanie walked up to take her part as lead policeman. A tear tugged at the corner of his eye. It seemed like just yesterday that his daughter took that very position. Now here was his precious granddaughter doing the same. At the proper signal, Stephanie marched forward down the aisle, up the steps, and onto the stage, secretly trying to see her parents in the audience. Yes, they were there beaming as proudly as could be.

"Only one more fund-raiser, and the year will be over," Kim told Tom late that evening after they had recounted their daughter's every move in the play.

"Yes, that is going to be hilarious," he said, grinning from ear to ear.

"I hope everyone has a good time," Kim commented. "A lot of people have put a lot of work into this talent show. There should be some good entertainment, and we should raise quite a bit of money for the youth group's trip to Georgia."

Kim's mother had planned a week-long trip for the youth group. She and Larry were going to take them to Atlanta, stopping to see many sites on the way there and back. A talent show was arranged to help them raise the money still needed for the trip.

"Your act with Gloria, Kelly, and Stephanie will get a laugh or two," Tom told her.

Stephanie and her friend Kelly were taking ballet lessons. Kelly's mom, Gloria, had been a friend of Kim's since grade school, and they decided it would be fun for their two daughters to perform at the talent show. But, being the instigators that they were, they planned to add a little twist to the act.

It was the night of the talent show. Stephanie and Kelly were the first to appear on stage as the music to "A Spoonful of Sugar Helps the Medicine Go Down" began. The curtains were closed, and there were sighs rippling through the auditorium as the two petite girls began their routine. Then a huge blast of laughter filled the air as Kim, who was five feet nine inches tall and heavy at the hips, and Gloria, who was much shorter than Kim, came bouncing out from behind the curtains in tutus. Yes, tutus of pink and black. They marched across the stage trying to learn the moves that their daughters were so elegantly making. Of course, the mothers could not catch on to the routines at all. They floundered and flapped across the stage until the dance was over. People laughed for a very long time.

The act was a huge success, as was the talent show. The children had all the money they needed for their trip.

Chapter Twenty-Nine

Tom and Kim enjoyed their time in Detroit and their activities at St. Matthew Church and School, but eventually they got tired of living in the big city. Since Kim no longer had her job, they were not tied to the area. They wanted to move to a small town. Midland, where Kim had been born, was a great choice. Not only was it a small town, but it was a family-oriented town that offered many opportunities to enjoy arts of all different types from music to paintings. Not far from the downtown area, which could easily compare to Mayberry, North Carolina, was a three-sided bridge called the Tridge. The parks that surrounded the Tridge were used constantly for picnicking, fishing, rollerblading or just relaxing. The area would be a great place for their family to live.

"Did your job transfer come through today?" Kim asked Tom after dinner one evening. Stephanie was in her room working on homework. Tom and Kim still sat at the dinner table.

"Yes, all of the paper work is done, and I start working at the new facility in six weeks," Tom informed Kim.

"Stephanie doesn't get out of school that soon," Kim reminded her husband.

"I know, but that is when the new Marriott opens. Even though I've enjoyed the last couple of years working for the Marriott down by the airport, I'm ready for a change. Working at a new hotel should be rewarding." As Tom explained the details of his job transfer to his wife, his mind wandered to thoughts of their impending move.

"Tom…" Kim called his name, bringing him back to the present.

"Sorry. I was just thinking how nice Midland is. I feel bad about taking Stephanie from her grandparents, but at least they go to Midland often to visit your grandparents."

"Don't worry. They'll come up often, and Stephanie can come down here and spend time too." Kim wanted Tom to be completely happy.

"That's true," Tom agreed.

"Why don't we tell her as soon as she's done with her homework," Kim suggested. Right about that time Stephanie walked into the room.

"Mom, I need help with spelling," the fifth grader announced.

"How can I help?" Kim asked.

"I have to know how to spell these ten words."

"Okay. Have a seat and I'll drill you." The attentive mother was happy to help.

"I'll do the dishes," Tom said, as he picked up the plates from the table.

Within just a few minutes, everyone was done with their jobs, so they moved to the living room. "Stephanie," Tom began, "Mom and I want to tell you something."

Stephanie was focused on her father's next words as he explained their plans and told her they would be moving as soon as school was out for the summer. Stephanie was very excited. She could hardly wait to tell her best friend, who lived three houses down from her. She took off running as soon as Tom finished the details.

Tom gave Kim a curious look. "Are you sure you are up to this?" he asked his wife.

"Yes." Kim told him. "The only residuals left from my heart surgery are the scar and the fact that I get tired more easily. Other than that, I do well as long as I pace myself."

The move went well. It was eight weeks later, and Kim was excited to share with Tom the events of the day. "Today I registered Stephanie at St. John's Lutheran School. They offer a great education, and the children there learn Bible verses just like Stephanie did at St. Matthew. Her teacher is even allowing her to continue in the same memory book she has been working from since kindergarten. I thought that was very kind of him."

"Wow! That's great. You got quite a bit done today." Tom encouraged his wife of thirteen years.

"If you'll bring up a few boxes from the basement, I'll work on them tomorrow."

"Said and done." Tom acquiesced to his wife's request and headed down the stairs to the basement to get the boxes.

The next morning Kim began unpacking one item after the other. As she reached down to the bottom of the box, she stopped suddenly. Something was happening. She couldn't move, and she could hardly breathe. Her heart felt as though it had stopped. She stood paralyzed for a few seconds. Then her heart gave a hard thump, and the episode was over.

Kim wondered what it was all about. She had never experienced this before. Did she need to see a cardiologist? No. That would be a hassle. She'd have to fill out the paperwork, wait in the office for the doctor, try to explain her heart condition, and get only the treatment she needed. Many doctors became so interested in her heart anatomy and listening to the swishing sound of her heartbeat that they forgot why she came. What should she do?

This is the first time something like this has happened, she thought. I'm probably working too hard. With those thoughts, she sat down to enjoy a television program and rest. She couldn't concentrate on the show. The heart problem kept gnawing at her. Should I call Tom and tell him? Should I call Mayo first and see if they have any idea what this could be? Should I make an appointment with a cardiologist here? These thoughts swirled and swirled through her mind. She couldn't seem to shake them.

Trying to escape her fears, she got up for a glass of Coke. With determination she decided to do nothing but wait and see if it happened again. She wasn't even going to tell Tom. He would just worry.

Several months went by without any other heart incidents. Tom and Kim's friend Cathy was in town for a week-long visit. They took her to see the Tridge, picnic in the park, and let her rollerblade down the Pere Marquette Rail-Trail, where the train tracks had been paved over for people to walk, ride bikes, and rollerblade.

On one particular afternoon, while Tom was at work and Stephanie was at school, Cathy and Kim were headed to the store. Kim was driving. They hadn't gotten very far when Kim had another episode. She slowly stopped the car and pulled off to the right.

"What's the matter?" Cathy asked, looking at Kim curiously.

Kim couldn't move. Her heart felt as though it had stopped again, and her vision was distorted. Everything appeared as though she were cross-eyed. All she could do was sit and wait for something to happen. Even though these episodes only lasted for a few seconds, it seemed like an eternity, because there was no way to tell what was going to happen next. Shortly her heart gave a hard thump, and everything went back to normal.

Scared, Kim asked Cathy to drive. Cathy looked at her, still puzzled about her friend's actions. "What happened?" she asked her close friend.

"Oh, this has occurred before. It's really strange, and I don't know exactly what it is. It feels as though my heart stops beating and I get paralyzed. I can't move. I just have to sit and wait for something to happen. Eventually my heart beats hard, and everything is fine."

"Have you called the cardiologist about it?" Cathy inquired.

"No. That was the first time it has happened in months." Kim tried to avoid Cathy's eyes.

"Have you told Tom?" Cathy knew her friend all too well.

"No, I will. I'll call Dr. Warnes on Monday to find out what she thinks. After I know what is going on, I'll tell Tom." Kim tried to make light of the situation, even though she was somewhat scared.

"Okay, but I'm going to call you next week and check to make sure you did," Cathy firmly informed her.

"All right." Kim understood that Cathy was right. This was nothing to ignore.

The following Tuesday Kim called her Mayo Clinic cardiologist. She got right through to the nurse and explained what happened. "I had another one a few months ago, but I thought I was just doing too much," she explained.

"Dr. Warnes is with a patient right now. I'll let her know what is going on, and one of us will give you a call this afternoon."

As predicted, Dr. Warnes called. "Hi, Mrs. Russell. This is Dr. Warnes. The nurse told me you are having some difficulties. Can you explain to me what happened?"

Kim began by telling Dr. Warnes about the first episode, which she had passed off as nothing. Then she went into a description of the second event. "At first I was worried that it was a stroke, but once my heart thumped, everything went back to normal." Kim was trying to give Dr. Warnes every bit of information she could.

"It's not a stroke. It sounds like some sort of heart rhythm problem. I don't think the distorted vision is related. I'll make a note in your chart. If it happens again, go to the closest emergency room and have them do an EKG."

"Okay, thank you for your help." Kim hung up the phone, relieved that it was not something serious enough to warrant an immediate trip to Mayo Clinic.

When Tom got home, Kim explained the entire story to him. "Why didn't you tell me?" He was upset that she hadn't shared something so important with him.

"Because I didn't think it was serious, which it wasn't. I didn't want you to worry." Kim tried to justify her actions.

Tom made his way across the room to hug his nervous wife. "Honey, you know we share everything. I only want to help you as much as possible."

"I know. I just don't want to be a burden unnecessarily."

"Kimberly Jean," Tom said firmly. "We are a family. We stick together no matter what. You need to tell me when you need help."

Kim looked down at the floor knowing he was right.

Kim, Tom, and Stephanie loved living in Midland. They enjoyed the benefit of the outdoor activities, the flare for the arts, and being close enough to visit Kim's grandparents and other relatives often. Her paternal grandparents lived in Midland, and her maternal grandfather lived only forty-five minutes away. Her aunts and uncles also lived close by.

"I love going out for breakfast with Grandma and Grandpa on Saturday mornings and having dinner with the whole family, including my parents on occasion," Kim told Tom on the way home from a local restaurant. "It is nice to spend time with them now since I didn't get to grow up around them."

"Yes, family is important," Tom agreed. "You know, we have enjoyed our time with your relatives, and it makes me wonder if we should move back to Atlanta. Stephanie deserves to be able to grow up around her cousins, aunts, and uncles. Now that my parents have moved back, it makes me want to be there."

Tom's words surprised Kim. He had been the one who had suggested they move to Midland in the first place. She thought living in a small rural town at a slower pace appealed to both of them. After a couple of minutes, Kim inquired about Tom's comment. "What are you saying? Do you want to move back to Atlanta?"

"Not right away, but we should at least think about it," he told her.

"Your point about Stephanie being able to live around her cousins and other family members does make sense. Let's think about it for a while." Kim encouraged her husband's desires.

After three months of thought and prayer, Tom and Kim put their house up for sale. By the end of their real estate contract, they had only showed their house a few times.

"Our contract will be up in a few weeks," Kim reminded Tom while they were walking through the grocery store. "We've had only a few people look at it. What do you make of that?"

"I don't know," Tom said. "What are we going to do?"

"I don't know either," Kim replied. "It's a nice house at a reasonable price. It should have sold by now." Over the next few days, Tom and Kim thought about what to do next…until they got the phone call the last week of the contract.

Tom answered the phone. "Hello?"

"Hi, Tom. Is Kim home? Can you both get on the phone?"

"Sure," Tom replied. He called Kim to pick up the other phone.

"Hello?" Kim answered with curiosity.

"Hi, Kim. It's Dad."

This caught Kim off guard. Usually her dad didn't call. She'd talk with him at the beginning or the end of a conversation with her mother. "Hi, how are you?" Kim asked.

"Fine, but I have some news," Larry replied.

Kim hesitated before responding. "What's going on?" she asked, not sure she wanted to know. It sounded serious.

"Grandpa Vinton has been diagnosed with lung cancer," Larry said, his voice cracking as he made the statement.

Tom and Kim stood staring at one another. "Is he going to be okay? What will happen?"

"I think you should go over and see him. He will tell you the details, but he didn't want to be the one to break the news."

Tears trickled down Kim's cheek. She and her grandfather had a special bond. "We'll call them and go over this afternoon," Tom answered, while Kim took hold of her emotions.

"Thanks for calling, Dad. We love you! Give Mom a hug from us." With that Tom and Kim hung up. Kim clung to Tom for a few minutes while she shed some tears. Then they made their way over to visit her grandparents.

Now the Russells knew why their house had not sold yet. God was keeping them here. Kim was not employed; she would be able to help take care of her grandfather. They had given him six to twelve months to live. She realized then why God had directed them to live in Midland.

About seven months into her grandfather's illness, his wife, Kim's grandmother, got up one night to get some water. No one knows how it happened, but she fell. An ambulance was called, and she was transported to the hospital, where she was diagnosed with a concussion. She only recognized a few people who came to visit, and by the next day she was in a coma. She died a week later. Grandpa Harley died three months after that, partly from cancer, but mostly from a broken heart. Kim and Tom were thankful that they had been able to spend so much of the last two and a half years with them.

The work of God's hand was obvious again. Three days after Grandpa Harley's death, a man came to their front door asking if they were still interested in selling their house. Two and a half months later, on January 31, they completed the sale of their house and moved to Atlanta.

Chapter Thirty

Living back in the Atlanta area took some adjustment—the fast pace, the hilly and curvy roads, and all of the new construction that had taken place while they had been gone. But being able to spend time with Tom's parents (Elizabeth and David Russell), his six brothers and sisters and their spouses, and his nieces and nephews was priceless. Kim's brother, sister, and their families were very close by also. The only ones who were not within the twenty-mile range were Kim's parents, who still lived in Michigan.

Stephanie settled into their new house easily. It was a nice house in a neighborhood with a swimming pool. She met friends at her parochial Lutheran school, but because the school was quite a distance from their house, Stephanie had a hard time meeting people in the area. Seeing her struggle some, Tom and Kim tried to convince her to participate in community activities.

"I don't want to do anything," Stephanie argued.

"Well, you can't just sit around the house," Kim urged.

"Mom's right, Stephanie. You have to do something. Here is a list of things to get involved in. Pick one, and we'll take you to get signed up." Tom offered his encouragement too.

"There is nothing on here that I want to do," Stephanie said, pouting because she knew it always got to her daddy's heart.

Tom stood firm. "Either you pick, or we'll pick, but you have to do something."

Stephanie huffed like a typical female teenager. Then she sat down on her bed. "I don't see anything I like," she answered, digging in a little harder.

"Okay. You're going to play softball. The tryouts are tomorrow. Be ready to leave here at three o'clock tomorrow afternoon." Tom spoke in a stern voice.

Another huff escaped Stephanie's lips. "Fine."

"And bring a good attitude," Tom demanded.

The next afternoon Stephanie whined all the way to the ball field. "I don't know why you're making me do this. I don't even know how to play on a real team. We just played for fun at St. Matthew. Plus, I don't even know anyone there." Strphanie went on whining.

"You'll be fine," both parents encouraged her.

As it turned out, Stephanie loved softball and met many new friends. The whole way home, she was excited about playing ball, telling Tom and Kim about everyone she met and her try-out efforts. She found out the next day that she made the team.

This was only the beginning of Stephanie's activity. Through softball she made many friends and met people her age in her neighborhood. She began participating in many activities—school functions, science projects, softball, and hanging out with her friends. She was busy all the time. In high school she played softball in the summer and volleyball in the winter. Time was passing quickly.

Tom and Kim sat reflecting on how Stephanie had adjusted to living in Atlanta. They were especially grateful for the time she had with her grandparents, aunts, uncles, and cousins. "Stephanie graduates in two weeks, doesn't she?"

"It's incredible how fast time can go. She has grown up to be a very special young lady, hasn't she?" Tom beamed with pride.

"Yes, she has. I am so proud of her and love her so much!"

"Me, too," Tom replied.

"Stephanie Renae Russell." As the high school principal called out the name, Stephanie crossed the stage to receive her diploma. She was already graduating from high school. Tears strolled down Kim's face. She thought back on the days when she was young and her health was uncertain, when she doubted she would ever find someone to marry. Now here she was. She was married and had a grown daughter who was graduating. Kim thought quietly to herself: God is good; I can't wait to find out what the rest of his plans are for me.

Chapter Thirty-One

"Stephanie is such a sweetheart, isn't she? She's really enjoying college in Minnesota." Kim made the comment to Tom as she ended her conversation with Stephanie and placed her cell phone back into her purse. The couple was enjoying the last day of their ten-day vacation in Michigan. They were driving down I-75 on the way back home to Atlanta.

"Yes," Tom agreed, as he merged into the left lane. "We have a great girl! Remember when she was in kindergarten and tried to take the cat to school in her book bag? She was so disappointed when I made her take it out." The couple began reminiscing about the fun years of parenthood.

Kim's face broke out into a grin.

"What?" Tom wanted to know why Kim was grinning.

"I was just thinking back on meeting some of her boyfriends, getting her ready for her first prom, and attending her graduation. Our baby girl is already" All of a sudden Kim's speech came to a complete halt. Her heart felt as though it had stopped, and she became totally still. All she could do was sit and wait to see what would happen next.

Fifteen to twenty seconds later, her heart thumped very hard and she could feel it start beating again. It took several minutes for all of her body to begin working normally again. It scared her.

Tom could tell what was happening. Kim had had these before, but this one was the longest and the worst. They were so far from one of the congenital heart doctors' offices. What should they do? Go to the nearest hospital, which was at the next exit? Going to a hospital that didn't know about Kim's heart condition would be scary. Wait and see what happens? By the time Tom went through these thoughts, Kim's symptoms were dissipating. Her body function was becoming normal again. She gave Tom a look that said "I don't know what that was, but it'll be okay" and motioned for him to keep driving. She would call Dr. Warnes when they got home.

The following Tuesday Kim decided it would be best to go to Emory for a checkup. She hadn't gone to Emory since their return to Atlanta. And now Dr.

Franch had retired. It was a real hardship to trust someone else with her care. At the same time, having a local cardiologist was now important. If she needed immediate care, where would she go?

Kim was nervous as she dialed the phone number for the congenital heart clinic at Emory. "I need to make an appointment," she stated. "I'm a patient there, but I have been going to Mayo Clinic for the last few years because that's where I had my last surgery."

"Are you coming in for a checkup?" the scheduler asked.

"No. I'm having some problems." Kim explained the episode she had a few days earlier.

"Can you hold, please?"

"Sure," Kim answered patiently.

"We can see you next Wednesday at 10:30 AM. Will that be okay for you?"

"Sure. Thank you. What is the doctor's name?"

"You will be visiting with Dr. Wendy Book and Dr. Michael McConnell."

"Okay," Kim answered. She knew Dr. Franch had retired, but to actually hear someone tell her that she would be seen by someone else was disappointing. Then a thought came to her. "Is Dr. Franch around there anymore?" Kim asked.

"Yes, he is. He sometimes comes in and works with the new congenital heart doctors on Wednesday." This announcement gave Kim hope.

"Will he be there next week?" She just had to know. Dr. Franch had been her mentor and confidant in cardiology for many years. It was so hard to let go and trust someone else.

"Probably, but I don't know for sure, because he does travel some."

"Okay. Thank you for your time." Kim ended the conversation and hung up the phone.

The following Wednesday Kim sat in the new cardiologist's office filling out paperwork. When she was done, the secretary took it and told her to have a seat. She didn't wait long.

"Kim Russell," the nurse called.

Kim got up and went across the room. "Lynn!"

The nurse smiled as she leaned over to give the heart patient a hug. "Yes, it's me. How are you? It's been a very long time since we hung out on the cardiac floor when you had endocarditis. You look great!"

Kim still couldn't believe she was actually talking to the nurse who had given her the special ring so long ago. She looked great and very happy. They stood for a few minutes reminiscing. Lynn filled her in on what some of the other nurses were up to and where they were working. It was great!

"I suppose we should get you into a room so we can take care of you," the nurse said, leading Kim down the hall to a room on the left. Lynn asked questions about the medical chart. Kim answered to the best of her ability.

"Is Dr. Franch here today?" Kim asked.

"Not today, but he does come in sometimes. I'll tell him you were here."

"Thanks."

Lynn finished the paperwork and questions. "Dr. Book will be with you shortly. If you need anything, just step into the hall and let us know."

Kim waited only a few minutes before the doctor entered. She came across the room and shook her new patient's hand. "Hi," she began. "I'm Dr. Book."

"Hi," Kim greeted her. "It's nice to meet you."

"So tell me what is going on," Dr. Book requested.

Kim went on to explain her history and her recent heart episodes. The female doctor paid close attention and asked a few questions. After jotting down a few notes, the cardiologist listened to her heart and lungs and excused herself. A few minutes later a technician walked in to do an EKG. Kim's mind wandered back to the EKGs she had in her childhood. How technology had advanced! From a ten-minute stay in a dark room, with straps on your arms and legs, to a few pads stuck on your legs, back, and neck for thirty seconds. Amazing!

After Kim dressed, Dr. Book took her to another room, where several people had gathered. "This is the other congenital cardiologist, Dr. McConnell." Dr. Book continued to introduce her to a couple nurses and a nurse practitioner.

"It's nice to meet all of you," Kim told them.

Dr. Book and Dr. McConnell talked to Kim about the episodes she had been having. Kim was so preoccupied with the fact that she was seeing new doctors and that something was wrong with her heart that she didn't fully comprehend everything said. She could only remember that they said something about her heart rhythm. When they finished, she was still somewhat clueless. "Will you call my cardiologist at Mayo Clinic?" Kim asked.

"Sure," both cardiologists told her. "We'll call her and let her know what is going on. She should have the test results by Friday. You could call her then and find out what she wants to do."

"Thank you." In one way Kim felt she was not being fair to these new cardiologists by not trusting them. At the same time, she knew Dr. Warnes had been caring for her for so many years. She was very familiar with her case.

Chapter Thirty-Two

Two days later Tom walked into the kitchen when he came home from work to find Kim on the phone. After giving her a hug and kiss, he gave Kim a perplexed look. "What are you doing?" he asked her.

"I'm calling Dr. Warnes about that episode I had in the car the other day. I want to find out what she thinks about the test results that Dr. Book faxed her and find out what I should do.

Kim turned back to the phone when someone answered. "Is Dr. Warnes in, please?" she asked politely.

The secretary asked for a message and told Kim to hold. A few minutes later the secretary's voice came over the phone again. "I have Dr. Warnes on the phone now," she informed Kim.

"Hi, Mrs. Russell. This is Dr. Warnes. How are you?"

Kim explained the medical incident to Dr. Warnes in detail. "Yes, Dr. Book sent me the test results," Dr. Warnes spoke thoughtfully. "You need to get treatment soon. Those arrhythmias can become fatal if you don't get them under control. There are medications to prevent them from happening. It takes a three-day hospital stay to introduce the medication to your system so your heart's response can be monitored. That can be done either here at Mayo Clinic or at Emory in Atlanta."

"Okay." Kim hesitated over the unexpected news. "My husband and I will talk about it over the weekend. I'll call you Monday morning."

Dr. Warnes approved the plan. "Make sure you call Monday morning."

"I will. Thank you for your help!"

Bright and early Monday morning, Kim called Dr. Warnes as promised. As soon as Dr. Warnes came on the line, Kim greeted her and began explaining her decision. "Tom and I have decided we want to come to Mayo for the treatment you and I talked about on Friday," she told her cardiologist. "You have been my heart-care giver for over ten years, and you know my heart best." Kim paused to take a breath before continuing. She and Tom had decided the best option was for them to travel to Mayo Clinic in three weeks, when Tom had an extra day off work.

Before Kim could even start explaining the plans, Dr. Warnes spoke. "Will you be coming here this afternoon or tomorrow morning?" she asked. The words took Kim by surprise. In a split second, she realized that Dr. Warnes was expressing the urgency of immediate care.

"This afternoon," Kim replied, still trying to grasp the reality of the situation.

"Good. I'll send the proper admission paperwork over to the hospital. Have them page me when you get there."

Thanks to their friend Heidi, who gave them buddy passes so they could fly inexpensively, Tom and Kim were soon on their way to Mayo Clinic in Rochester, Minnesota.

As soon as Kim and Tom were in Kim's hospital room, the nursing staff began the needed treatments. An IV was inserted, her chest was decorated with small round patches for the heart monitor, and her nurse began explaining the therapy she was about to receive. "Patients are hospitalized for close observation during the loading of Amiodarone to monitor heart rate and rhythm.

"During the next couple days, you will be going for a liver function test, a thyroid study, a pulmonary function test, and an eye exam. This medication can, in four to seven years, have an adverse effect on any of these areas. A baseline chart will help determine if there is any change as time goes on." The whole time the nurse talked, she worked.

"We are also starting you on Coumadin, which is a blood thinner. This will keep the blood pumping through your heart at just the right consistency."

The nurse hooked up the medication to the IV. As she did, Dr. Warnes' words echoed through the patient's mind: "Make sure that if you ever have an IV, no matter where you are, you have a double filter. We cannot afford to get any air into your bloodstream."

Kim looked up at the nurse in concern. "Did you put a double filter on my IV line?" she asked.

The hospital worker looked at her. "Yes. That is what the doctor ordered."

Immediately after the nurse completed her work and left the room, Dr. Warnes walked in. "Hello!" she said. "I see we already have the medication flowing. How is that going?"

Kim smiled. She was always comforted and encouraged by Dr. Warnes' presence. "The nurse just left. So far it is going well."

Dr. Warnes crossed the room and inspected the intravenous line. "Did they put two filters on the tubing?"

"Yes, they did," Kim informed the cardiologist, confirming that the doctor had properly trained her.

"Have they explained what will happen over the next three days?" Dr. Warnes asked.

"Yes." Kim explained to Dr. Warnes all that the nurse had told her, including the tests that would be run and the possible effects of the medication.

"Good." Dr. Warnes seemed satisfied with her patient's knowledge. "I'll be popping in from time to time to check on you, and a regular medical doctor will visit with you twice a day. If you have any questions or concerns, please ask either of us."

"Okay," Kim agreed.

On her way out the door, Dr. Warnes tapped Kim on the toes. "Keep those legs uncrossed. It can cause blood clots."

Kim uncrossed her legs and watched her cardiologist walk out the door. Tom sat in the corner with a smirk on his face. "She always catches you doing that, doesn't she." Kim was not amused.

The three days of Amiodarone and Coumadin therapy and the tests passed without event. In fact, they were boring. Because Kim was on a heart monitor, she could only walk through the hallway immediate to her room. She and Tom spent every day sitting in the room watching television or walking the same hallway up and down.

On the third day, Dr. Warnes came by Kim's room to release her from the hospital. "Just make sure you follow the orders written on your dismissal papers. Study your new diet guidelines and your INR levels now that you are taking Coumadin. Read again all of the information the nurse gave you, and keep it readily available in case you need to refer to it. You will need to see Dr. Book next week for a follow-up visit. Do you have any questions?"

Tom and Kim both shook their heads. "No."

"Then I'll be on my way. It was great to see you again. Take care of yourself, and I'll see you in a year. Your dismissal papers will be ready in about half an hour." Dr. Warnes shook their hands and walked out the door.

As soon as Dr. Warnes left the room, Tom called to make the flight arrangements for the trip home.

Chapter Thirty-Three

Two years passed by quickly and with only a couple minor cardiac events. Kim was still visiting Mayo Clinic once a year, but she also kept in close touch with Emory. She was getting to know the cardiologists there. They were building her confidence in their abilities. Dr. Franch's presence at many of her visits helped.

In the meantime, Stephanie moved back home from college. She decided she would work during the day and go to school at night. Within a year of being home, she met Mr. Right, Matthew Faithauer. She and a group of friends had gone to New York for New Year's Eve on Time Square. She had captured the attention of the young man who had served them dinner. Within six months he had moved to the Atlanta area.

Tom was watching TV and Kim was working in the office on the computer when the doorbell rang. Kim heard Tom go to the door to answer it. "Kim," he called out, "you need to come in here." Kim came down the hallway and spotted Matt. Immediately she knew what was happening. "Let's sit down on the couch," Tom suggested.

The three of them went into the living room to sit down. Matt wasted no time in making his intentions known. He loved Stephanie and wanted to marry her. "I didn't come to get your permission, Mr Russell. I want your *blessing*, and I won't ask her until I get it."

Tom and Kim were in a state of shock. Tom spoke first. "We have some things to discuss first," Tom began. "The most important thing is that you know what she believes. I think it would be a good idea if you took Bible classes before asking her. A house built on two foundations cannot stand."

Matt nodded his head. "That is one of the things that I like most about Stephanie. She knows what she believes and sticks to her doctrine no matter what."

Kim broke in quietly. "Don't you think it is kind of soon? Ya'll have been dating for only eight months." Kim stopped short and quit talking. She remembered that she and Tom knew they would get married after only two weeks. Her argument held absolutely no water.

Tom continued. "You need to think about how you are going to support her. She is used to being well taken care of."

Matt's disappointment was obvious. He thought that Stephanie's parents did not consider him good enough for her. Slowly he took the purchase papers for Stephanie's ring out of his top pocket and handed them to Tom. "Here," he said. "These are the papers I need to pick up Stephanie's ring. When you think I am ready, please give them back to me."

After hugging both parents, he left through the front door.

Tom and Kim met in the kitchen still somewhat stunned. "Well, what do you think?" Tom asked.

"I think I was not prepared for that, and perhaps we didn't do a good job. The issue of the Christian faith had to be addressed, and I do think Matt should take the classes at church. They should get counseling first. At the same time, they are adults. They're old enough to know what they are doing. They are twenty-two and twenty-five. We were only twenty and twenty-four."

"Good point," Tom said. "If he was willing to come and ask for our blessing, that says a lot."

"Right," Kim said. "I'm sorry that I wasn't much help to you. Maybe we should call him and let him know it is okay."

"Let's think on this until morning and decide what to do," Tom recommended.

The next evening Tom and Kim had Matt come back over. Tom started the conversation. "Matt, we've never been in this position before, and we didn't handle last night very well. We're sorry. You know what is important to Stephanie, and we trust you to take good care of her both physically and spiritually. We appreciate the fact that you were willing to wait until you had our blessing. You have our blessing." Tom finished as he handed the papers back to his future son-in-law.

Matt took the papers and hugged Tom and Kim. "Thank you." He stalled for a few seconds. "Stephanie knows. I couldn't keep it from her because I was so upset last night."

"We can work something out, Kim interjected. "You'll be able to surprise her when you give it to her." Right about that time Matt's cell phone rang. Grinning, he looked up.

"It's Stephanie," he said, as he clicked the answer button. "Hi, Honey. No. I'm still at your parents' house. Yeah, we talked. They want to get together tomorrow morning for breakfast and make sure we are all in agreement about a few things." Matt was wearing a most devious grin. "I'm leaving here in just a few minutes."

Kim and Tom were laughing. "That was easy, wasn't it?" Kim giggled.

"Yeah. This is going to be fun!" Matt chuckled.

Later that evening Kim called Stephanie. "Hi, Honey. How are you?"

"I'm doing as well as I have been doing all day," Stephanie huffed. "Nothing is going right. I gotta go." Kim hung up quickly. It was obvious that Stephanie was blaming them for not being engaged yet. You'll find out soon enough, Dear, Kim thought with a smile on her face.

That night Stephanie and Matt were at a party. As they sat out on the deck at their friend's house, Matt swung himself onto one knee in front of her. "Stephanie, will you marry me?" With that he pulled out the ring to put on her finger.

Stunned, Stephanie let out an excited yelp. "What are you doing?"

"I'm asking you to marry me. Your parents gave us their blessing today, but I didn't want you to know. I wanted to surprise you."

"Well, you did a good job!"

"But you haven't answered my question."

Stephanie gave him a blank stare. "What?"

"Will you marry me?"

"Yes! Yes!" she replied, jumping up from her chair. They gave each other a hug and went inside to tell their friends the news.

"Aren't you going to call your parents?" Matt asked her.

"Oh, no, I'm not. Two can play the 'I've got a secret game.'"

The next morning when the four met for breakfast, Tom and Kim arrived first. They were anxious to see if Matt had proposed yet. When Stephanie and Matt pulled up, Stephanie was digging through her purse in search of something.

"Good morning, Stephanie," Kim called out to her.

Stephanie looked up with a beam in her eyes, but she was still digging. Kim knew then that Stephanie was playing a game with her. "All right," Kim said, pausing for effect. "Let's see it!"

Stephanie pulled her hand out of her purse. On her finger was one of the most beautiful engagement rings Kim had ever seen. There was a large diamond in the middle, with sapphires and diamonds lining the band on either side. The family hugged and went in to eat breakfast.

Epilogue

Five months later, on January 14, 2006, Matt and Stephanie were joined in marriage. It was a special service. Stephanie's grandfather married them and delivered a beautiful sermon on marriage, reminding the young couple that marriage was about being selfless.

"It's hard to believe that those five months of planning are over and Stephanie is married," Kim said to Tom one evening in April as they sat reflecting.

"And it was so beautiful." Tom expressed his satisfaction with the whole ordeal. "I can't tell you how many people commented that it was simply elegant and how nice it was that your dad performed the ceremony for his own granddaughter." Tom paused. "That is pretty special!"

"That was special!" Kim agreed. "Our guests seemed to appreciate that it was a marriage ceremony and not just a wedding."

Tom looked down at his wife. "I think it was as special as our own wedding day, just in a different way. That was almost twenty-five years ago."

Tom and Kim sat staring at the floor, their minds wandering to other special events in their lives. "We've had a lot of great times in our life together, haven't we?" Tom commented thoughtfully.

Kim beamed at her husband's sweet words. She could hardly believe what a miraculous life God had given her. From the time she was able to understand her condition, she had wondered how long she would live. Here she was at age forty-six, looking back on her high school graduation; wedding; adoption of their precious little girl; and her warm, loving relationship with her husband of twenty-five years. "Yes, we have had a lot of fun. A lot of fun! We've had some rough times too, but God has taken such good care of us. I thank him mostly for giving you to me. You have been wonderful to me! You've always been there for me in every situation. No matter what I've wanted to accomplish or do, you have always been right there with me. During my surgery and illnesses, you held my hand to comfort, encourage, and support me. Thank you for all you've been!"

Tom leaned over and kissed Kim on the forehead. "I love you!"

"I love you too, Dear!" Kim answered.

Shifting his weight on the couch and turning Kim's head toward him, Tom leaned over and looked her directly in the eyes. "Do you know *why* I love you?"

Supposing it to be a rhetorical question, Kim did not reply, but she waited for his explanation. "First of all, I love you for you. Second, life is never dull. I enjoy the things we do together, whether it is volunteering at Camp Braveheart, playing cards at the senior-living apartments, or serving at church. A new experience or adventure seems to be waiting around each corner. All during the preparation of Stephanie's wedding in January, you told me time and time again that as soon as the wedding was over you were going to concentrate on finishing your book. Two weeks before the wedding, you got an e-mail from the Adult Congenital Heart Association, and the next thing I knew, you were preparing to go to Washington D.C. You were home from D.C. only a few days when you got another e-mail asking you to attend the American College of Cardiology Conference in downtown Atlanta to help work the Adult Congenital Heart Association booth. In the meantime, you are helping to plan the 2006 Camp Braveheart week and working on your book."

Kim just smiled at him, knowing that he was right. The last six months had been full of exciting events, one right after another.

"Oh," Tom continued, "did I mention about the adventure of being on a Fox News report about Emory University and their congenital heart clinic that you participated in? And I believe that just last week you helped the 11Alive television station honor your retired cardiologist, Dr. Franch. You never cease to amaze me!"

Kim smiled. She was thrilled to be involved in every one of these projects. It was awesome. And Tom was always right there by her side to help. "Well, there has been a lot going on, but I wouldn't be able to live a full life like that without *you*. You are always right there beside me with your love, encouragement, and support." Kim started to tear up. "Honey, thank you for all you do for me! I love you so very much!" The two embraced in a big hug that would last a lifetime.

Bibliography

Everett, Allen D, and Lim, D. Scott. *Illustrated Field Guide to Congenital Heart Disease and Repair.* Second edition. Charlottesville, Virginia: Scientific Software Solutions, Inc., 2005. www.PedHeart.com

Gersh, Bernard J., M.D., editor-in-chief. Mayo Clinic Heart Book: The Ultimate Guide to Heart Health. Second edition. New York: William Morrow and Company, Inc., 2000. www.mayoclinic.org/cardiacsurgery-rst/

Lam, Conrad R., M.D. Archives Collection. Detroit, Michigan.

Helpful Web Sites

Adult Congenital Heart Association
www.achaheart.org
This Web site has a list of camps for children with congenital heart conditions. There is a list of support groups for adults with congenital hearts throughout the United States.

Adult Congenital Heart Clinic in Atlanta
www.emoryhealthcare.org

Children's Healthcare of Atlanta
www.choa.org

Children's Heart Foundation
www.childrensheartfoundation.org

Congenital Heart Information Network
www.tchin.org

Kids with Heart
www.kidswithheart.org

Mayo Clinic Congenital Heart
www.mayoclinic.org/congenital-heart

The author loves to hear from her readers. You may contact her at Kim@Kimsheartbeat.com or visit her website www.KimsHeartbeat.com.

978-0-595-39771-6
0-595-39771-9

Printed in the United States
201258BV00003B/1-186/A